OPPOSING
VIEWPOINTS®
SERIES

US Foreign Policy

Other Books of Related Interest

Opposing Viewpoints Series

Afghanistan

Illegal Immigration

Syria

World Peace

At Issue Series

Does the World Hate the US?

Drones

Is Foreign Aid Necessary?

Should the US Close Its Borders?

Current Controversies Series

Immigration

Pakistan

Politics and Religion

Racial Profiling

"Congress shall make no law . . . abridging the freedom of speech, or of the press."

First Amendment to the US Constitution

The basic foundation of our democracy is the First Amendment guarantee of freedom of expression. The Opposing Viewpoints series is dedicated to the concept of this basic freedom and the idea that it is more important to practice it than to enshrine it.

OPPOSING VIEWPOINTS® SERIES

US Foreign Policy

Noël Merino, Book Editor

GREENHAVEN PRESS
A part of Gale, Cengage Learning

GALE
CENGAGE Learning·

Farmington Hills, Mich • San Francisco • New York • Waterville, Maine
Meriden, Conn • Mason, Ohio • Chicago

GALE
CENGAGE Learning®

Patricia Coryell, *Vice President & Publisher, New Products & GVRL*
Douglas Dentino, *Manager, New Products*
Judy Galens, *Acquisitions Editor*

LIBRARY OF CONGRESS CATALOGING-IN-PUBLICATION DATA

US foreign policy / Noël Merino, book editor.
    pages cm -- -- (Opposing viewpoints)
    Includes bibliographical references and index.
    ISBN 978-0-7377-7296-8 (hardback) -- ISBN 978-0-7377-7297-5 (paperback)
    1. United States--Foreign relations. 2. World politics--21st century. I. Merino, Noël, editor of compilation. II. Title: U.S. foreign policy. III. Title: United States foreign policy.
    JZ1480.U79 2014
    327.73--dc23
                                                        2014024606

Printed in the United States of America
1 2 3 4 5   19 18 17 16 15

Contents

Chapter 1: What Are Some Criticisms of US Foreign Policy?

Chapter 2: Are Foreign Military Interventions Good for the United States?

Chapter 3: Are US Economic Policies Worldwide Good for the United States?

Chapter 4: What Considerations Should Guide the Future of US Foreign Policy?

Why Consider
Opposing Viewpoints?

> *"The only way in which a human being can make some approach to knowing the whole of a subject is by hearing what can be said about it by persons of every variety of opinion and studying all modes in which it can be looked at by every character of mind. No wise man ever acquired his wisdom in any mode but this."*
>
> *John Stuart Mill*

In our media-intensive culture it is not difficult to find differing opinions. Thousands of newspapers and magazines and dozens of radio and television talk shows resound with differing points of view. The difficulty lies in deciding which opinion to agree with and which "experts" seem the most credible. The more inundated we become with differing opinions and claims, the more essential it is to hone critical reading and thinking skills to evaluate these ideas. Opposing Viewpoints books address this problem directly by presenting stimulating debates that can be used to enhance and teach these skills. The varied opinions contained in each book examine many different aspects of a single issue. While examining these conveniently edited opposing views, readers can develop critical thinking skills such as the ability to compare and contrast authors' credibility, facts, argumentation styles, use of persuasive techniques, and other stylistic tools. In short, the Opposing Viewpoints Series is an ideal way to attain the higher-level thinking and reading skills so essential in a culture of diverse and contradictory opinions.

In addition to providing a tool for critical thinking, Opposing Viewpoints books challenge readers to question their own strongly held opinions and assumptions. Most people form their opinions on the basis of upbringing, peer pressure, and personal, cultural, or professional bias. By reading carefully balanced opposing views, readers must directly confront new ideas as well as the opinions of those with whom they disagree. This is not to argue simplistically that everyone who reads opposing views will—or should—change his or her opinion. Instead, the series enhances readers' understanding of their own views by encouraging confrontation with opposing ideas. Careful examination of others' views can lead to the readers' understanding of the logical inconsistencies in their own opinions, perspective on why they hold an opinion, and the consideration of the possibility that their opinion requires further evaluation.

Evaluating Other Opinions

To ensure that this type of examination occurs, Opposing Viewpoints books present all types of opinions. Prominent spokespeople on different sides of each issue as well as well-known professionals from many disciplines challenge the reader. An additional goal of the series is to provide a forum for other, less known, or even unpopular viewpoints. The opinion of an ordinary person who has had to make the decision to cut off life support from a terminally ill relative, for example, may be just as valuable and provide just as much insight as a medical ethicist's professional opinion. The editors have two additional purposes in including these less known views. One, the editors encourage readers to respect others' opinions—even when not enhanced by professional credibility. It is only by reading or listening to and objectively evaluating others' ideas that one can determine whether they are worthy of consideration. Two, the inclusion of such viewpoints encourages the important critical thinking skill of objectively evaluating an author's credentials and bias. This evaluation will illuminate an author's reasons for taking a particular stance on an issue and will aid in readers' evaluation of the author's ideas.

It is our hope that these books will give readers a deeper understanding of the issues debated and an appreciation of the complexity of even seemingly simple issues when good and honest people disagree. This awareness is particularly important in a democratic society such as ours in which people enter into public debate to determine the common good. Those with whom one disagrees should not be regarded as enemies but rather as people whose views deserve careful examination and may shed light on one's own.

Thomas Jefferson once said that "difference of opinion leads to inquiry, and inquiry to truth." Jefferson, a broadly educated man, argued that "if a nation expects to be ignorant and free . . . it expects what never was and never will be." As individuals and as a nation, it is imperative that we consider the opinions of others and examine them with skill and discernment. The Opposing Viewpoints series is intended to help readers achieve this goal.

David L. Bender and Bruno Leone,
Founders

Introduction

"Peace, commerce, and honest friendship with all nations, entangling alliances with none."

—President Thomas Jefferson,
Inaugural Address, 1801

One of the main functions of the federal government is to conduct relations on an international level with other countries. US foreign policy has evolved over time, reflecting changes in the nation's interests, priorities, and goals. As a military and economic superpower, the United States today has a foreign policy distinct from the policy of 120 years ago, illustrating how foreign policy evolves and changes in response to the nation's place in the world and its leadership position.

During the nineteenth century, the United States was focused on building a nation. One goal influencing foreign policy was the desire to enlarge the nation, prompting agreements such as the Louisiana Purchase from France in 1803 and the purchase of Florida in 1819 from Spain. President James Monroe articulated his approach to foreign policy to Congress in 1823 in what came to be known as the Monroe Doctrine. The main concepts of the doctrine were that (1) the United States would not interfere with the affairs, wars, or existing colonies of Europe and (2) the Western Hemisphere was not available for future colonization, and any attempt by a European nation to control any nation in the Western Hemisphere would be viewed as a hostile act against the United States. The doctrine signified a distinct break from Europe and enunciated the nation's interests in non-colonization and non-intervention.

Just prior to the beginning of the twentieth century, the United States lost its aversion to interventionism and decided to intervene in the Cuban War of Independence, thereby launching the Spanish-American War and, shortly thereafter, the Philippine-American War. After these wars, America turned inward again, embracing neutrality during the first three years of World War I, until it entered as an "associate" of the Allies under President Woodrow Wilson. At the end of the war, the United States failed to join the League of Nations, which would have given war powers of the US government to the league's council.

The United States turned inward again in the 1920s and 1930s. Franklin D. Roosevelt announced his so-called Good Neighbor Policy during his inaugural address in 1933: "In the field of world policy I would dedicate this nation to the policy of the good neighbor—the neighbor who resolutely respects himself and, because he does so, respects the rights of others." The new policy reflected the priority on domestic concerns, in no small part the result of the economic problems of the Great Depression.

Despite a series of neutrality acts passed in the late 1930s to keep the United States out of international conflict, the United States entered World War II in 1941. After the end of the war, the United States used economic assistance as a strategic element of its foreign policy and, unlike the experience with the League of Nations, became one of the first members of the United Nations. In response to security concerns created by World War II and the ensuing Cold War, the National Security Act of 1947 was passed, providing for a secretary of defense and creating the National Security Council.

The ensuing decades saw several US military interventions, cementing the US position in the world as a military superpower. Two of these major interventions had the goal of containing communism. The 1950s brought US troops to fight for South Korea in the Korean War; and in the 1960s and

1970s, US troops supported South Vietnam against Communist North Vietnam. Despite failures to eliminate communism in North Korea and North Vietnam, the United States saw an end to the Cold War, the fall of the Berlin Wall, and the dissolution of the Communist Soviet Union in the 1980s. The collapse of the Soviet Union in 1991 left the United States as arguably the sole superpower in the world, increasing expectations of peace while simultaneously increasing expectations of US military and economic interventions worldwide when needed.

Beginning at the end of the twentieth century and continuing into the twenty-first century, US foreign policy began to focus on the Middle East, not only because of concerns about protecting access to oil but also because of security concerns in the region. The Gulf War of 1991 and the wars in Iraq and Afghanistan were the notable military operations of the last few decades, pursued with varying degrees of coalition forces. The last few decades, however, also have seen several humanitarian interventions, such as the foreign aid and troops sent to Somalia, peacekeeping efforts during the war in Bosnia, and restoration of order in Haiti.

Over time, US foreign policy has shifted among varying degrees of isolationism, interventionism, engagement, and humanitarianism. In *Opposing Viewpoints: US Foreign Policy*, authors take a variety of viewpoints on the subject of current foreign policy in chapters titled "What Are Some Criticisms of US Foreign Policy?," "Are Foreign Military Interventions Good for the United States?," "Are US Economic Policies Worldwide Good for the United States?," and "What Considerations Should Guide the Future of US Foreign Policy?" The divergent viewpoints of this volume illustrate the wide disagreement about the role of the United States in the world and the debate about the principles that ought to guide US foreign policy.

OPPOSING
VIEWPOINTS®
SERIES

CHAPTER 1

What Are Some Criticisms of US Foreign Policy?

Chapter Preface

The United States faces criticism both domestically and internationally for its foreign policies. One issue of controversy both within and from the outside regards the notion of American exceptionalism. At the *National Review Online*, the president of the Foundation for Defense of Democracies Clifford D. May defines American exceptionalism as the "recognition that America is, as James Madison said, the 'hope of liberty throughout the world,' and that America is different from other nations in ways that are consequential for the world." Just how much this notion of American exceptionalism ought to inform foreign policy—if at all—is the subject of widespread debate.

Part of the debate about exceptionalism depends on how it is defined. Opinion writer Richard Cohen notes in the *Washington Post*, "American exceptionalism ought to be called American narcissism. We look perfect only to ourselves." But senior fellow at the Center for Individual Freedom Troy Senik disagrees, arguing, "American exceptionalism is not the same as American perfectionism. It does not hold the nation to be an infallible vessel of God's own will. Rather, it simply notes that America has traveled farther and faster than any nation in history toward the conditions that maximize human flourishing—and that it has done so because of the unique nature of its ideology and the unique character of its institutions."

President Barack Obama spoke of how American exceptionalism affects US foreign policy in his September 10, 2013, speech on Syria: "America is not the world's policeman. Terrible things happen across the globe, and it is beyond our means to right every wrong. But when, with modest effort and risk, we can stop children from being gassed to death and thereby make our own children safer over the long run, I believe we should act. That's what makes America different.

That's what makes us exceptional." Russian president Vladimir Putin responded in the *New York Times*, taking Obama's call of American exceptionalism to be a denial of equality: "It is extremely dangerous to encourage people to see themselves as exceptional, whatever the motivation. There are big countries and small countries, rich and poor, those with long democratic traditions and those still finding their way to democracy. Their policies differ, too. We are all different, but when we ask for the Lord's blessings, we must not forget that God created us equal."

Historian Bernard Weisberger writes of the foreign policy dangers of a belief in American exceptionalism at *Moyers & Company*:

> At a time when we need the world's friendship and cooperation, the exceptionalist mind-set licenses administrations of both mainstream parties to override the sovereignty of other nations in the interests of our own safety.... Think of the symbolic impact of our refusals to sign international treaties banning the use of land mines or child soldiers, or of the special exemptions we demand from prosecution by local law authorities of crimes committed against civilians by our military personnel in the countries where we have bases established. What kind of self-portrait are we painting?

However, Ramesh Ponnuru at the *National Review Online* argues that American exceptionalism leads to special responsibilities in the world:

> Our country has always been exceptional. It is freer, more individualistic, more democratic, and more open and dynamic than any other nation on earth. These qualities are the bequest of our founding and of our cultural heritage. They have always marked America as special, with a unique role and mission in the world: as a model of ordered liberty and self-

government and as an exemplar of freedom and a vindicator of it, through persuasion when possible and force of arms when absolutely necessary.

Exceptionalism aside, the following chapter demonstrates that there are those who defend US foreign policy decisions and those who criticize the role the United States has in the world.

> *"Support for U.S. global engagement,*
> *already near a historic low, has fallen*
> *further."*

Americans Want Less Global Military Involvement and More Economic Involvement

Pew Research Center for the People and the Press

In the following viewpoint, the Pew Research Center for the People and the Press contends that a recent survey shows that a majority of the American public believes the United States plays a less important role globally and should mind its own business internationally. The author claims that Americans' top foreign policy goals largely reflect domestic concerns, even as a large majority believes preventing terrorist attacks is the top priority. The Pew Research Center for the People and the Press provides independent public opinion survey research about American attitudes toward politics and policy.

As you read, consider the following questions:

1. What percentage of Americans say the United States is less respected than in the past, according to the viewpoint?

2. What fraction of the American public, according to the author, says that Iran's nuclear program is a major threat to the well-being of the United States?

3. According to the author, what percentage of Americans believe President Barack Obama is not tough enough in his approach to foreign policy and national security issues?

Growing numbers of Americans believe that U.S. global power and prestige are in decline. And support for U.S. global engagement, already near a historic low, has fallen further. The public thinks that the nation does too much to solve world problems, and increasing percentages want the U.S. to "mind its own business internationally" and pay more attention to problems here at home.

A Shift in Public Opinion

Yet this reticence is not an expression of across-the-board isolationism. Even as doubts grow about the United States' geopolitical role, most Americans say the benefits from U.S. participation in the global economy outweigh the risks. And support for closer trade and business ties with other nations stands at its highest point in more than a decade.

These are among the principal findings of America's Place in the World, a quadrennial survey of foreign policy attitudes conducted in partnership with the Council on Foreign Relations (CFR), a nonpartisan membership organization and think tank specializing in U.S. foreign policy.

The survey of the general public, conducted Oct. 30–Nov. 6 [2013] among 2,003 adults, finds that views of U.S. global importance and power have passed a key milestone. For the first time in surveys dating back nearly 40 years, a majority (53%) says the United States plays a less important and powerful role as a world leader than it did a decade ago. The share saying the U.S. is less powerful has increased 12 points since 2009 and has more than doubled—from just 20%—since 2004.

An even larger majority says the U.S. is losing respect internationally. Fully 70% say the United States is less respected than in the past, which nearly matches the level reached late in former president George W. Bush's second term (71% in May 2008). Early last year [January 2012], fewer Americans (56%) thought that the U.S. had become less respected globally.

A Skepticism About International Engagement

Foreign policy, once a relative strength for President [Barack] Obama, has become a target of substantial criticism. By a 56% to 34% margin, more disapprove than approve of his handling of foreign policy. The public also disapproves of his handling of Syria, Iran, China and Afghanistan by wide margins. On terrorism, however, more approve than disapprove of Obama's job performance (by 51% to 44%).

The public's skepticism about U.S. international engagement—evident in America's Place in the World surveys four and eight years ago—has increased. Currently, 52% say the United States "should mind its own business internationally and let other countries get along the best they can on their own." Just 38% disagree with the statement. This is the most lopsided balance in favor of the U.S. "minding its own business" in the nearly 50-year history of the measure.

After the recent near miss with U.S. military action against Syria, the NATO [North Atlantic Treaty Organization] mission in Libya and lengthy wars in Afghanistan and Iraq, about half of Americans (51%) say the United States does too much in helping solve world problems, while just 17% say it does too little and 28% think it does the right amount. When those who say the U.S. does "too much" internationally are asked to describe in their own words why they feel this way, nearly half (47%) say problems at home, including the economy, should get more attention.

Support for Involvement in the Global Economy

But the public expresses no such reluctance about U.S. involvement in the global economy. Fully 77% say that growing trade and business ties between the United States and other countries are either very good (23%) or somewhat good (54%) for the U.S. Just 18% have a negative view. Support for increased trade and business connections has increased 24 points since 2008, during the economic recession.

By more than two to one, Americans see more benefits than risks from greater involvement in the global economy. Two-thirds (66%) say greater involvement in the global economy is a good thing because it opens up new markets and opportunities for growth. Just 25% say that it is bad for the country because it exposes the U.S. to risk and uncertainty. Large majorities across education and income categories—as well as most Republicans, Democrats and Independents—have positive views of increased U.S. involvement in the world economy.

To be sure, the public sees some harmful consequences from the movement of companies and people across borders. A majority (62%) says that more foreign companies setting up operations in the United States would mostly help the economy. But 73% think that the economy would be hurt if more U.S. companies move their operations abroad.

The public has mixed views of the impact of attracting more high-skilled and low-skilled people from other countries to work in the United States: 46% say more high-skilled workers from abroad would mostly help the economy while 43% see benefits from increasing the number of low-skilled workers from other countries.

Views of Council on Foreign Relations Members

A companion survey of 1,838 members of the Council on Foreign Relations (CFR), conducted online from Oct. 7–Nov. 11, provides a unique perspective on public attitudes about America's place in the world. The organization's members have a decidedly internationalist outlook: For example, majorities see benefits for the United States from possible effects of increased globalization, including more U.S. companies moving their operations overseas.

The CFR members, who were enthusiastic about Barack Obama's presidency four years ago, offer some significant criticism today. More than four in ten (44%) say Obama's handling of foreign policy is worse than they expected, while just 16% say it is better than expected; 40% say it met their expectations. A particular area of disappointment stands out among the CFR members: that Obama's handling of the situation with Syria weakened America's reputation around the world.

Notably, there is consensus among the organization's members that the public has become less internationalist. Fully 92% say that in recent years "the American public has become less supportive of the U.S. taking an active role in world affairs."

When asked why the public has become less supportive of global engagements, 42% of CFR members point to the wars in Iraq and Afghanistan, or explicitly cite "war fatigue." About a quarter (28%) mention the struggling U.S. economy or the costs of international engagement. Other factors cited are the ineffectiveness of recent U.S. interventions (mentioned by 19%) and failures of U.S. leadership (17%).

The Public's Opinion About Iran

The surveys, which were completed before the multilateral agreement aimed at freezing Iran's nuclear development pro-

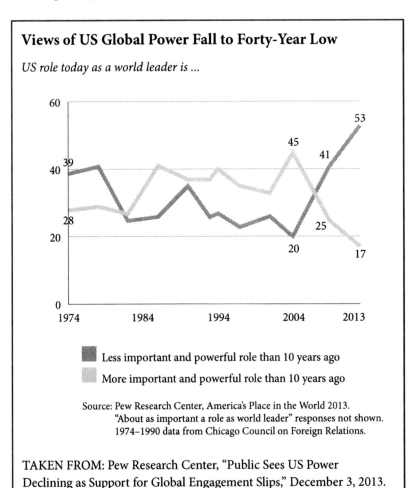

Views of US Global Power Fall to Forty-Year Low

US role today as a world leader is ...

Less important and powerful role than 10 years ago

More important and powerful role than 10 years ago

Source: Pew Research Center, America's Place in the World 2013.
"About as important a role as world leader" responses not shown.
1974–1990 data from Chicago Council on Foreign Relations.

TAKEN FROM: Pew Research Center, "Public Sees US Power
Declining as Support for Global Engagement Slips," December 3, 2013.

gram, find that most Americans do not believe that Iranian leaders are serious about addressing concerns over its nuclear program. Among those who heard at least a little about the nuclear talks, just 33% say they think Iranian leaders are serious about addressing international concerns about the country's nuclear enrichment program, while 60% say they are not.

Members of the Council on Foreign Relations have more positive views of Iranian leaders' intentions. Still, just half

(50%) of the organization's members say Iranian leaders are serious about addressing concerns over its nuclear program, while 44% disagree.

Among the public, there are partisan differences over whether Iranian leaders are serious about addressing concerns over the country's nuclear program. Majorities of Republicans (73%) and Independents (62%) who have heard at least a little about the nuclear talks say Iranian leaders are not serious in addressing nuclear concerns. Democrats who have heard about this issue offer more mixed evaluations; 42% say Iranian leaders are serious and 48% say they are not.

Iran's nuclear program continues to be one of the top global threats to the United States in the public's view. Nearly seven in ten Americans (68%) say that Iran's nuclear program is a major threat to the well-being of the United States, which has changed only modestly from America's Place in the World surveys in 2009 and 2005.

The Public's Views of Global Security Threats

Views of other long-standing global threats, such as Islamic extremist groups like al Qaeda (75% major threat), North Korea's nuclear program (68%) and China's emergence as a world power (54%), also have changed little in recent years.

However, the public now is deeply concerned by an emerging security threat, possible cyber-attacks against the United States. Seven in ten (70%) say that cyber-attacks represent a major threat, placing this on par with Islamic extremist groups and Iran's nuclear ambitions.

In terms of China and Russia, in particular, the public does not view either country very favorably—just 33% have a favorable opinion of China while 32% view Russia favorably.

Yet there is no evidence of growing public alarm about either China or Russia. Only about one in five Americans (23%) regard China as an adversary, while 43% see the country as a serious problem but not an adversary; 28% say China is not much of a problem. That opinion has held fairly steady for more than a decade. Similarly, relatively few (18%) view Russia as an adversary; 36% say Russia is a serious problem but not an adversary and 40% think the country is not much of a problem.

When asked which country represents the greatest danger to the United States, identical percentages volunteer Iran and China (16%). Nearly one in ten (9%) say that the United States itself represents the greatest danger, while 7% each cite North Korea and Iraq.

The Public's Top Foreign Policy Priorities

As in the past, many leading foreign policy priorities reflect domestic concerns. While 83% say that protecting the United States from terrorist attacks should be a top long-range foreign policy goal, about as many (81%) rate protecting the jobs of American workers as a top priority.

Majorities also say that reducing the country's dependence on imported energy sources (61%) and combating international drug trafficking (57%) should be top priorities, while nearly half say the same about reducing illegal immigration (48%).

Many of the public's domestically oriented goals are not shared by most members of the Council on Foreign Relations: Just 29% say protecting the jobs of American workers should be top policy priority, compared with 81% of the public. And only about one in ten CFR members (11%) sees reducing illegal immigration as a top long-range policy goal; 48% of the public views reducing illegal immigration as a top priority.

Climate change stands out as an issue of greater priority to CFR members than the public: A majority of the organization's members (57%) say that dealing with global climate change should be a top foreign policy goal, compared with 37% of the public.

Promoting human rights abroad, helping improve living standards in developing countries and promoting democracy rate as relatively low priorities for both the public and CFR members. These views have changed only modestly in recent years.

The Perceptions of U.S. Global Power

In the public's view, China long ago surpassed the United States as the world's top economic power. In the new survey, 48% say China is the world's leading economic power while just 31% say it is the United States. That is little changed from recent years.

Yet, most Americans (68%) continue to say that the United States is the world's leading military power. Just 14% think China has overtaken the United States in military strength.

In general terms, however, an increasing share of Americans think that the United States plays a less important and powerful role as world leader than it did 10 years ago. Currently 53% see the U.S. as a less powerful world leader, up from 41% in 2009.

Members of the Council on Foreign Relations also believe that U.S. power has declined. A majority of the organization's members (62%) express this view, compared with 44% in 2009.

Partisan Differences in Opinion

Partisanship is a major factor in changing public opinion about U.S. global power. Nearly three-quarters of Republicans (74%) say the United States plays a less important and powerful role than it did 10 years ago, up from 50% four years ago and just 8% in July 2004.

Yet, the percentage of political Independents who view the U.S. as less powerful also has grown, from 23% in 2004 to 45% in 2009 and 55% today. Democrats' views have changed little over this period; in the current survey, 33% of Democrats say the U.S. is less powerful than it was a decade ago.

Partisan differences are not as pronounced in opinions about whether the United States is respected internationally. Majorities of Republicans (80%), Independents (74%) and Democrats (56%) say the United States is less respected by other nations than in in the past.

In contrast with attitudes about America's global power, there is more partisan agreement that the United States should be less active internationally. About half of Independents (55%) and Republicans (53%) and 46% of Democrats say the United States should mind its own business internationally. In 2002, following the 9/11 attacks [referring to the September 11, 2001, terrorist attacks on the United States], 27% of Independents, 22% of Republicans and 40% of Democrats wanted the United States to mind its own business internationally.

The Public's Opinion on Obama and Foreign Policy

Barack Obama's overall job approval rating has fallen over the past year, and he gets low ratings for his handling of a number of foreign policy issues. His job rating is below 40% for nine of 10 foreign policy issues tested, including his overall handling of the nation's foreign policy. Terrorism is the only issue on which more approve of the job he is doing (51%) than disapprove (44%).

Views of Obama's job performance in handling foreign policy issues are mostly on par with ratings of his performance on some domestic issues. The survey finds that 37% approve of the way Obama is handling health care and just 31% approve of his handling of the economy.

About half of Americans (51%) say that Obama is not tough enough in his approach to foreign policy and national security issues; 37% say his approach is about right while 5% say he is too tough. The share saying Obama is not tough enough has risen 10 points since September (from 41%), though it is only slightly higher than the percentage describing him this way in April 2010 (47%).

With regard to specific security policies, 50% say the use of military drones to target extremists in Pakistan and other countries in the region has made the United States safer from terrorism, just 14% say it has made the U.S. less safe, while 27% say it has not made a difference.

The government's phone and Internet surveillance programs get mixed grades: 39% say they have made the nation safer from terrorism, 14% less safe and 38% say they have not made a difference. Finally, as the war in Afghanistan is winding down, just 31% of the public say the 12-year-long conflict has made the country safer from terrorism, 21% say it has made the U.S. less safe, and the plurality view (43%) is that it has not made a difference in U.S. security.

| "*Majorities across the political spectrum support the U.S. taking an active role in world affairs.*"

The Majority of Americans Want the United States to Be More Active in World Affairs

Gregory Holyk and Dina Smeltz

In the following viewpoint, Gregory Holyk and Dina Smeltz argue that most Americans want the United States to take an active role in world affairs, with Republicans supporting this view more than Democrats and Independents. The authors claim that most Americans view Iran, the Middle East, and China as focal points of US foreign policy but differ on their level of concern and opinions of how to handle foreign affairs. Holyk is a research analyst at Langer Research Associates, and Smeltz is a senior fellow in public opinion and foreign policy at the Chicago Council on Global Affairs.

As you read, consider the following questions:

1. According to the authors, which political group has the highest proportion of members finding strong US leadership in world affairs highly desirable?

2. Among Democrats, Independents, and Republicans, which group most favors staying out of a conflict between Israel and Iran, according to the authors?

3. According to the authors, among Democrats, Independents, and Republicans, who views China as a rival and who views China as a partner?

While majorities across the political spectrum support the U.S. taking an active role in world affairs, more self-described Republicans (70%) support taking an active role than Democrats (60%) and Independents (55%). Support for taking an active part in world affairs among Independents has dropped 15 points over the past decade, compared to only 7 and 10 points among Republicans and Democrats, respectively, over that same time span.

One of the clearest ways to differentiate the foreign policy views of Democrats and Republicans is to identify which foreign policy goals they see as very important. Democrats are more apt to see limiting climate change, combating world hunger, strengthening the United Nations [UN], and defending human rights as "very important" foreign policy objectives by double-digit margins, while Republicans are more likely to see great importance in reducing illegal immigration, maintaining U.S. military power, and combating terrorism. In most cases, these differences are ones of intensity and not opposing majorities.

Republicans are also less likely than others to support defense budget cuts, though a majority still favor cuts (54% of Republicans, vs. 76% of Democrats and 71% of Independents). Finally, the proportion of those calling strong U.S. leadership in world affairs "very desirable" is highest among Republicans (45%), while smaller proportions of Democrats (35%) and Independents (28%) share that view.

Views on Afghanistan and Pakistan

While majorities across partisan lines do not think the U.S.-led war in Afghanistan has been worth the costs and do not think the war has made the United States safer from terrorism, Republicans are less negative than Democrats and Independents. GOP [Grand Old Party, referring to the Republican Party] backers are also more likely to want to leave some combat troops in Afghanistan after 2014 (28% Republicans, 11% Democrats, 16% Independents) and more likely to be "very concerned" about the threat to American national security if the Taliban returned to power in Afghanistan (46%, vs. 37% of Democrats and 33% of Independents).

As in the past, Republicans view the world in terms of power and security to a greater degree than Democrats and Independents. Accordingly, Republicans are more likely than Democrats and Independents to view terrorism (77%, vs. 65% of Democrats and 61% of Independents), Islamic fundamentalism (54%, vs. 31% of Democrats and 35% of Independents), and Islamist groups in Afghanistan and Pakistan (65%, vs. 52% of Democrats and 44% of Republicans) as critical threats to U.S. vital interests.

Democrats and Independents are more supportive of non-military approaches to foreign policy such as diplomatic engagement and foreign aid. Democrats and Independents are more open to talking with the leaders of the Taliban and other unfriendly countries or non-state actors, and are more inclined to make joint decisions within the UN [United Nations] (66% of Democrats and 57% of Independents, vs. 43% of Republicans).

While fewer than half of all respondents favor maintaining or increasing economic aid to Afghanistan and Pakistan, Democrats are more favorable towards aid for both countries. Nearly half of Democrats support increasing economic aid to Afghanistan (45%, 32% Republicans, 36% Independents);

about a third of Democrats support increasing aid to Pakistan (36% Democrats, 22% Republicans, 31% Independents).

Views on Israel and Iran

Americans view Iran and its nuclear ambitions as one of the most critical threats to the United States, but partisanship colors how Americans think Washington should handle Iran. Broad majorities across all three groups support economic sanctions and diplomacy. Only Republicans, though, reach majority support for United Nations authorization of a military strike against Iranian nuclear energy facilities (58% vs. 41% of Democrats and Independents alike).

If Israel and Iran were to go to war following an Israeli strike on Iranian nuclear facilities, a majority of Democrats (66%) and Independents (65%) favor the United States staying out of the conflict, while a majority of Republicans (54%) favor the United States entering the conflict on the side of Israel.

The Changing Middle East

Americans remain apprehensive about threats from the Middle East, with most Americans (73%) viewing the region as the source of the greatest security threats to the United States in the future. One of the key questions for American foreign policy in this region has been whether or not conflict between Islam and "the West" is inevitable. On this topic, Republicans are much more pessimistic than Democrats and Independents. A majority of Republicans (56%) say that "because Muslim social and political traditions are incompatible with Western ways, violent conflict between the two civilizations is inevitable." In contrast, majorities of Democrats and Independents (58% each) say that "because most Muslims are like people everywhere, we can find common ground and violent conflict between the civilizations is not inevitable."

Overall, Americans are mixed about whether the Arab Spring [a revolutionary movement that began in 2010 and

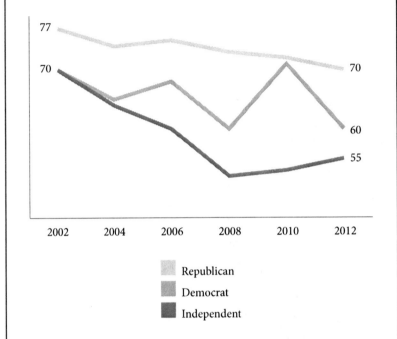

Americans' Views on World Affairs

Percentage who think it will be best for the future of the country if we take an active part in world affairs.

Legend:
- Republican
- Democrat
- Independent

TAKEN FROM: Gregory Holyk and Dina Smeltz, "Background Brief for Final Presidential Debate: What Kind of Foreign Policy Do Americans Want?," Chicago Council Survey, October 19, 2012.

spread throughout the Arab world] will be good or bad for the United States (34% mostly good, 37% no impact, 24% mostly bad). Its reverberations continue to be felt in the Middle East, nowhere more so than in Syria, where Americans support limited action. Six in ten support increasing economic and diplomatic sanctions against the Syrian regime (63%), and nearly as many support enforcing a no-fly zone over Syria (58%). Beyond these options, there is limited support for sending arms and supplies to antigovernment groups in Syria (27%), bombing Syrian air defenses (22%) or sending troops into Syria (14%). Support for these actions crosses partisan affiliation: Majorities among Republicans, Democrats and Independents all support economic and diplomatic sanctions and a no-fly zone and oppose other options.

Support for actions against terrorism remains strong even as it has declined among all political groups in the decade since the September 11 attacks. Yet Democrats and Republicans continue to differ slightly in their preferred approaches. Higher percentages of Democrats support working with the United Nations and helping poor nations economically over air strikes on terrorist sites and the assassination of terrorist leaders, while more Republicans support air strikes and assassination than working through the UN or helping poor nations. Majorities from both parties, however, support all these measures. While lesser majorities from both parties support attacks by ground troops against terrorist encampments, more Republicans than Democrats are willing to take such action.

The Rise of China

Long focused on Europe, Americans have slowly come to see Asia as an increasingly important region to the United States. For the first time in Chicago Council [on Global Affairs] surveys going back to 1994, when asked which continent is more important to the United States—Asia or Europe—slightly more Americans (52%) say that Asia is more important than say Europe is more important (47%). Democrats and Independents are more likely than Republicans to say that Asia is more important to the United States than Europe (54% and 56%, respectively, vs. 45% of Republicans). However, despite the Democrats' greater relative focus on Asia, the shift in priorities from Europe to Asia over the past ten years has been apparent across the political spectrum.

There is little doubt among Americans that China's economy will one day grow as large as that of the United States. But Republicans are more worried about this prospect than others, with 49 percent saying it would be a negative development, compared with 38 percent of Democrats and 37 percent of Independents. In addition, a slight majority of Republicans (51%) and Independents (53%) see China as a rival, while a majority of Democrats (54%) see it as a partner. Although Republicans may be more wary of China, majorities across the partisan spectrum say the United States should pursue a policy of friendly engagement and cooperation with China.

China is not the only rising power in the world: Countries like Turkey and Brazil are becoming increasingly independent in the conduct of their foreign policies. A large majority of Americans (69%) see this as mostly a good thing because it makes them less reliant on the United States. This view is shared across party lines by majorities of Democrats (73%), Republicans (69%), and Independents (66%) alike.

> "The American veto policy of uncondi-
> tional support for illegal Israeli prac-
> tices must end."

The United States Should Stop Shielding Israel

Ibrahim Sharqieh

*In the following viewpoint, Ibrahim Sharqieh argues that the
United States needs to change its approach in dealing with Israel
from one of accommodation to one of assertive diplomacy. Sharqieh claims that US protection of Israel from international pressure by vetoing resolutions on settlement construction has the
potential to lead to the end of peace prospects and the dangerous
collapse of the Palestinian Authority. Sharqieh is a foreign policy
fellow at the Brookings Institution, the deputy director of the
Brookings Doha Center, and an adjunct professor at Georgetown
University's School of Foreign Service in Qatar.*

As you read, consider the following questions:

1. According to Sharqieh, what was the international
   community's hope in adopting an approach of accommodation in dealing with Israel?

2. Where does the author suggest the stirrings of a Palestinian Spring may be occurring?

3. The author suggests that the United States refuse to provide diplomatic cover for Israel's dangerous, unproductive moves, such as what?

We are now [January 2013] set for a third term for Israeli premier Benjamin Netanyahu. And, although Netanyahu's Likud Yisrael Beiteinu coalition seems to have underperformed expectations, a plurality of the vote will allow him to once again lead Israel's government.

U.S. Accommodation of Israel

But even a somewhat moderated Netanyahu government will continue to advance radical positions that put regional and global security in danger. The question, then, is how the United States can best push another right-wing administration to behave in accordance with the principles of the international security system—and its own national interests.

Over the past two Netanyahu terms, the international community, and the United States in particular, adopted an approach based on accommodation when dealing with the Netanyahu government. The hope was that this approach would contain the risks this extremist government posed to international security. Yet just as that strategy did not work then, it will not work now. The United States must therefore now take a harder line with Israel's coming government—it must switch from a strategy of accommodation to one of confrontation, and it should start by letting fall its diplomatic shield.

In order to protect Israel from international pressure, the United States has repeatedly vetoed U.N. [United Nations] Security Council resolutions that criticize Israeli government actions—including resolutions on settlement construction that the United States itself publicly rejects. In return, Netanyahu

© Jehad Awrtani/Cartoonstock.com.

has publicly flouted American priorities. Europe has also accommodated the Netanyahu government. In exchange, Netanyahu refused a request from German chancellor Angela Merkel, his strongest European ally, to temporarily freeze settlement construction. The negotiating "Quartet," meanwhile, has yielded to the Israeli government's position since its inception. The Quartet—made up of the United States, Russia, the European Union, and the United Nations—was repaid in last January's Amman talks. It requested that each negotiating party submit in writing its vision for final status talks; while the Palestinians complied, Netanyahu declined, dealing the Quartet a humiliating defeat.

The Potential for Negative Consequences

This international forbearance has tipped the already skewed balance of power between Israel and the Palestinians and essentially left Israel with no incentive to negotiate or compromise. A Netanyahu-led Israel whose military, economic, and now diplomatic power dwarfs that of the Palestinians no longer sees any reason to be part of a sustainable solution.

Continuing to enable the latest iteration of the Netanyahu government threatens a host of dangerous, unpredictable consequences. Netanyahu's plans to continue settlement expansion will effectively put an end to peace efforts in the region. Just Tuesday [January 22, 2013], British foreign secretary William Hague said that Israel's settlement policy "will make a two-state solution impossible." Now, a further deterioration of peace prospects could produce the long-overdue "Palestinian Spring." We may see the first stirrings of this sort of mass, nonviolent protest in Bab al-Shams and Bab al-Karama—two tent cities that have sprung up to obstruct Israeli expansion plans in the occupied West Bank. More dangerously, though, settlement growth will likely lead to the collapse of the Palestinian Authority, something the United States has gone to great lengths to protect and support. The vacuum left by the authority's implosion could lead to a surge of violence, which may seem to many Palestinians like their only legitimate alternative. The same void would effectively invalidate the Quartet's reason for existence—and even require direct international intervention to restore order. And all this is to say nothing of the possibility Netanyahu could drag the United States into a new region-spanning war with Iran, just as America is winding down its long, costly wars in Iraq and Afghanistan.

Of course, there is now reason to think that Israel's ironclad international support may be changing. Europe made an obvious and historic shift in its diplomacy when its member states either voted yes or abstained in the recent United Nations vote on Palestinian statehood. President [Barack] Obama's nomination of Chuck Hagel as secretary of defense, coupled with his refusal to withdraw the nomination in the face of sharp opposition, also suggests a possible policy evolution. Obama has entered his second term with a freer hand on foreign policy. Hagel's antiwar positions and his openness to dialogue with Iran imply that Obama may be willing to challenge Netanyahu at some point; if so, he will have European and international backing.

The Need for Assertive Diplomacy

The Obama administration has leverage, and it should use it. Further accommodation of Netanyahu and his right-wing policies will only exacerbate the already complicated and difficult issues underlying the Palestinian-Israeli conflict.

The United States has to draw the line sometime—and that time should be now. It can start by practicing more assertive diplomacy, namely by refusing to provide diplomatic cover for dangerous, unproductive moves—settlement expansion is only one example. If Netanyahu wants to continue on this road, he must understand that he'll have to do so alone. The American veto policy of unconditional support for illegal Israeli practices must end, and, like the Europeans, the Obama administration must let Benjamin Netanyahu face the consequences of his own policies.

By letting slip its diplomatic shield, the United States can leave behind a failed policy of accommodation. In doing so, it can once again provide hope for a just, sustainable solution to the Palestinian-Israeli conflict, and at the same time protect its national interests in the Middle East.

> *"Today, especially, when Washington lacks a reliable Arab partner ... Israel and Saudi Arabia are critically important."*

Does America Still Have a Special Relationship with Israel and Saudi Arabia? And, If So, Is It Even Worth Keeping?

Aaron David Miller

In the following viewpoint, Aaron David Miller argues that the special relationships the United States has with Saudi Arabia and Israel are vitally important. Miller claims that the value of stability in the region is important enough for the United States to overlook differences and maintain the countries as allies. Furthermore, Miller argues that the three countries actually have shared interests with respect to Iran and Egypt. Miller is the vice president for new initiatives and a distinguished scholar at the Woodrow Wilson International Center for Scholars.

Aaron David Miller, "Does America Still Have a Special Relationship with Israel and Saudi Arabia? And, If So, Is It Even Worth Keeping?," *Foreign Policy*, October 31, 2013.

As you read, consider the following questions:

1. According to the author, who was president when the United States developed its special relationship with Saudi Arabia?

2. According to Miller, what did a March 2013 Gallup poll reveal about American sentiment toward Israel?

3. What example does the author give of an advantage to come from the US relationship with Saudi Arabia?

A week or so ago, I found myself sitting on a panel about Iran with Saudi Prince Turki bin Faisal Al Saud and Israel analyst and former Mossad officer Yossi Alpher.

If F. Scott Fitzgerald was right that the mark of the sophisticated mind is the ability to reconcile the yes and the no, he should have been there to see this. The Israeli-Saudi exchanges were fascinating, cordial, edgy, and quite instructive. There was some real push and pull on the Israeli-Palestinian issue, but clearly a common view on the danger and challenge posed by Iran.

As a historian by training though not by trade, the Israeli-Saudi conversation started me thinking about these two U.S. allies—how they agreed and disagreed with one another and we with them. But most of all, I was reminded how primary they both have been and still are to America's successes and failures in the Middle East.

During the 1940s when the United States was first getting its feet wet in the Middle East (and its oil), Washington developed very special, though very different, relationships with Riyadh and Jerusalem, roughly about the same time. The first with Saudi Arabia was driven largely by the growing importance of oil in the wake of World War II and the European recovery. Nothing was more emblematic of that emerging relationship than the famous meeting between President Franklin D. Roosevelt and Saudi King Abdul Aziz on Great Bitter Lake in February 1945. And while Roosevelt was likely as enamored by kings and the romance of distant and exotic lands as he was by Middle East strategy, the basis would be laid for a strategic relationship lubricated by Saudi oil in exchange for U.S. security guarantees and military, technological, and economic support for the kingdom.

A more complex mix of moral, humanitarian, and domestic political concerns would drive U.S. support for the creation of a Jewish state in the wake of the Nazi Holocaust. And a bit of realpolitik, too. By the spring of 1948—with the newly created State of Israel coming into being—President Harry Truman saw merits in adviser Clark Clifford's arguments that the Russians were poised to recognize Israel and that Washington shouldn't worry much about Abdul Aziz's reaction. The Saudis, he argued, had nowhere else to sell their oil and no one else to help them develop it. Clifford turned out to be right, for the most part. Indeed with rare exceptions, notably the 1973 Arab oil embargo, the United States has succeeded in keeping oil and Palestine quite separate.

Over the years, these two special relationships would continue to develop, mature, and to define much about U.S. policy in the region. Indeed, of the three original reasons for America's involvement in the Middle East—the Cold War, oil, and Israel—only the last two really continue to shape U.S. policy. Regardless of differences between the United States and these two strange Middle East bedfellows, what binds the bilateral ties has been stronger than what divides them. And this is likely to continue. To bring Mark Twain into the argument, rumors of their demise have been greatly exaggerated. More than likely they're here to stay. And here's why.

Stability, Stability, Stability

It is the cruelest of ironies that with all of the promise of the Arab Spring and its tropes of democratization, gender equality, freedom of conscience, and the like, it is the authoritarian kings, Saudi Arabia in particular—the anti-force to all of these values—that have survived largely untouched. And this administration and its predecessor—for all the talk of the Freedom Agenda and being on the right side of history—still values stability as the paramount virtue. The Saudis don't want an Arab Spring in Riyadh. And neither does Washington.

Sure, there are tensions in the relationship, and yes the oil-for-security trade-off has been weakened. But billions in arms sales and oil technology, the U.S. commitment to Gulf security, and bases and prepositioning in Gulf Cooperation Council countries nearby continue to drive the importance of this relationship. Whatever doubts the Saudis have about U.S. reliability, should Iran or anyone else threaten the kingdom, they won't be calling Moscow or Beijing first for help.

As for the U.S.-Israel relationship, the character of that bond remains as durable as ever. It's in the broadest conception of the American national interest to support like-minded democracies and that value affinity remains the bulwark of the relationship. Just take a look at the March 2013 Gallup poll revealing that public support for Israel is at an all-time high. Since the Arab Spring, that bond has only strengthened as Israel's Arab neighbors have melted down—driving spikes in violence, anti-American sentiment, and anti-Semitic rhetoric.

The fact remains that Israel's best talking points in Washington in defense of a strong relationship remain the Arab instability and dysfunction that mark their neighborhood. It would take a fundamental change in America's image of Israel to break that bond. And part of that change would require an [Anwar] Sadat–like Arab leader to make the case in a way that few Arab leaders have ever done, at least since the death of Jordan's King Hussein.

The Bizarre Axis of Common Enemies

No two countries could be more fundamentally different in character, history, religious affiliation, political system, and culture than Israel and Saudi Arabia. The old joke that when the Jews left Egypt Moses should have turned right instead of left and everything might have been different puts the matter in perspective. That the United States has managed to maintain these relationships and benefit from them without much conflict given the differences between them is as much a result of basic Saudi and Israeli needs as it was American diplomatic creativity and skill.

Still, rarely, if ever, it seems have Israeli and Saudi interests seemed to converge as closely as they do now, leaving the United States on certain issues the odd man out. Of course, there are major differences over the pursuit of Arab-Israeli peace. But on issues relating to Egypt (where Riyadh and Jerusalem welcome the military's return), and Iran (where both fear a nuclear Tehran) it may well be that this informal Jerusalem-Riyadh axis carries more influence than one may think, particularly on the Iranian nuclear issue. The United States will be hard-pressed to do a deal with Iran that leaves two of its last remaining Middle East allies angry, aggrieved, and fundamentally left doubting America's will and power. And so most likely, despite Saudi and Israeli fears, Washington probably won't be forced to accept its own stated slogan that no deal is better than a bad one. Two allies in hand is worth one very problematic potential frenemy in the proverbial bush.

But that leaves us with a big question: Are these special relationships even good for Washington anymore? The argument has been made for years that the United States is too subservient to Israel and too addicted to Saudi oil. Why not reduce its dependence on these two and make new friends? How about Turkey? Maybe even Iran? Surely, building these relationships would help the United States be seen as more credible around the region. One could argue it would also allow it greater freedom of action to protect its interests. There's no doubt that maintaining close ties with the specials come with liabilities. Washington is directly linked to supporting or acquiescing in Israeli policies toward the Palestinians and other Arabs that engender rage, and support for the Saudi monarchy makes a mockery of U.S. principles of democracy and respect for human rights.

But for seven decades now, the advantages of these relationships have also made America relevant and influential in a very tough region. In war and in peace, these relationships have proved invaluable. When Saddam [Hussein] invaded Kuwait, the Saudis offered vital staging areas and Arab cover to enable the United States to push him out. And without the U.S. relationship with Israel, there would have been no Egyptian-Israeli peace treaty and likely no chance of an Israel-Palestine peace agreement today either.

But the U.S.-Israel relationship is supposed to be special—not exclusive. And America is still too dependent on Saudi oil and not nearly tough in pushing the kingdom to stop funding jihadi groups and Wahhabi ideology.

Yet today, especially, when Washington lacks a reliable Arab partner, when it can't seem to make up its mind as to whether Egypt is a friend or adversary, Israel and Saudi Arabia are critically important. There are clear differences in these bilateral ties; but these really do pale compared with the convergence. If the White House wants to manage the Iran nuclear issue or push the Israel-Palestine peace process forward or keep trying to find a solution for Syria, it needs their help. With friends like these, many critics of the special relationships argue, who needs adversaries? But the critics tend to see the world as they want it to be, not the way it is. But with diminished U.S. influence and perhaps even a reduced role in the region, can beggars be choosers? Who else are we really going to rely on? This really isn't Lehman Brothers. We have them; and they're too big to fail.

| "The current trajectory of U.S. drone strike policies is unsustainable."

The Increasing Use of Drone Strikes Demands International Regulation

Micah Zenko

In the following viewpoint, Micah Zenko argues that the existing drone strike practices by the United States carry risks for US interests. Zenko claims that criticism of the limited transparency of current targeted killings by drones threatens the future existence of any use of drones. Additionally, Zenko contends that there is a risk of drone proliferation. Zenko concludes that the United States, along with other international actors, should develop a normative framework for drone strikes. Zenko is the Douglas Dillon Fellow in the Center for Preventive Action at the Council on Foreign Relations.

As you read, consider the following questions:

1. According to Zenko, how many drones are part of the US military's inventory?

2. The author proposes that the United States limit targeted killings by drones to which people only?

3. Zenko claims that reforming drone strike policies will allow the United States to sustain international cooperation needed to carry out future drone strikes, giving what two examples?

O ver the past decade, the use of unmanned aerial systems—commonly referred to as drones—by the U.S. government has expanded exponentially in scope, location, and frequency. From September 2001 to April 2012, the U.S. military increased its drone inventory from fifty to seventy-five hundred—of which approximately 5 percent can be armed. Yet despite the unprecedented escalation of its fleet and missions, the U.S. government has not provided a clear explanation of how drone strikes in non-battlefield settings are coordinated with broader foreign policy objectives, the scope of legitimate targets, and the legal framework. Drones are critical counterterrorism tools that advance U.S. interests around the globe, but this lack of transparency threatens to limit U.S. freedom of action and risks proliferation of armed drone technology without the requisite normative framework.

The Risks of Current Drone Policy

Existing practices carry two major risks for U.S. interests that are likely to grow over time. The first comes from operational restrictions on drones due to domestic and international pressure. In the United States, the public and policy makers are increasingly uneasy with limited transparency for targeted killings. If the present trajectory continues, drones may share the fate of [George W.] Bush–era enhanced interrogation techniques and warrantless wiretapping—the unpopularity and illegality of which eventually caused the policy's demise. Internationally, objections from host states and other counterterrorism partners could also severely circumscribe drones' effec-

The US Drone Program

American drones have been sent to spy on or kill targets in Iran, Iraq, Afghanistan, Pakistan, Yemen, Syria, Somalia and Libya. Drones routinely patrol the Mexican border, and they provided aerial surveillance over Osama bin Laden's compound in Abbottabad, Pakistan. In his first three years, [President Barack] Obama has unleashed 268 covert drone strikes, five times the total George W. Bush ordered during his eight years in office. All told, drones have been used to kill more than 3,000 people designated as terrorists, including at least four U.S. citizens. In the process, according to human rights groups, they have also claimed the lives of more than 800 civilians. Obama's drone program, in fact, amounts to the largest unmanned aerial offensive ever conducted in military history; never have so few killed so many by remote control.

Michael Hastings,
"The Rise of the Killer Drones:
How America Goes to War in Secret,"
Rolling Stone, April 16, 2012.

tiveness. Host states have grown frustrated with U.S. drone policy, while opposition by non-host partners could impose additional restrictions on the use of drones. Reforming U.S. drone strike policies can do much to allay concerns internationally by ensuring that targeted killings are defensible under international legal regimes that the United States itself helped establish, and by allowing U.S. officials to openly address concerns and counter misinformation.

The second major risk is that of proliferation. Over the next decade, the U.S. near monopoly on drone strikes will erode as more countries develop and hone this capability. The advantages and effectiveness of drones in attacking hard-to-reach and time-sensitive targets are compelling many countries to indigenously develop or explore purchasing unmanned aerial systems. In this uncharted territory, U.S. policy provides a powerful precedent for other states and non-state actors that will increasingly deploy drones with potentially dangerous ramifications. Reforming its practices could allow the United States to regain moral authority in dealings with other states and credibly engage with the international community to shape norms for responsible drone use.

The Need for Reform

The current trajectory of U.S. drone strike policies is unsustainable. Without reform from within, drones risk becoming an unregulated, unaccountable vehicle for states to deploy lethal force with impunity. Consequently, the United States should more fully explain and reform aspects of its policies on drone strikes in non-battlefield settings by ending the controversial practice of "signature strikes"; limiting targeted killings to leaders of transnational terrorist organizations and individuals with direct involvement in past or ongoing plots against the United States and its allies; and clarifying rules of the road for drone strikes in non-battlefield settings. Given that the United States is currently the only country—other than the United Kingdom in the traditional battlefield of Afghanistan and perhaps Israel—to use drones to attack the sovereign territory of another country, it has a unique opportunity and responsibility to engage relevant international actors and shape development of a normative framework for acceptable use of drones.

Although reforming U.S. drone strike policies will be difficult and will require sustained high-level attention to balance transparency with the need to protect sensitive intelligence sources and methods, it would serve U.S. national interests by

- allowing policy makers and diplomats to paint a more accurate portrayal of drones to counter the myths and misperceptions that currently remain unaddressed due to secrecy concerns;

- placing the use of drones as a counterterrorism tactic on a more legitimate and defensible footing with domestic and international audiences;

- increasing the likelihood that the United States will sustain the international tolerance and cooperation required to carry out future drone strikes, such as intelligence support and host-state basing rights;

- exerting a normative influence on the policies and actions of other states; and

- providing current and future U.S. administrations with the requisite political leverage to shape and promote responsible use of drones by other states and non-state actors.

As [Barack] Obama administration officials [such as John O. Brennan] have warned about the proliferation of drones, "If we want other nations to use these technologies responsibly, we must use them responsibly."

"The historical record of international agreements in keeping the peace and limiting carnage is weak."

The Drone Wars: International Law Will Not Make Them Humane

Arthur Herman and John Yoo

In the following viewpoint, Arthur Herman and John Yoo argue that concerns about drones should be addressed by new technology, not by international regulation. The authors claim that past efforts to contain new innovations with regulation have failed, even sometimes disadvantaging democracies. Herman and Yoo contend that deterrence and counter-technologies are better strategies for addressing concerns about the use of drones. Herman is a visiting scholar at the American Enterprise Institute, and Yoo is a professor at the University of California, Berkeley, School of Law.

As you read, consider the following questions:

1. Herman and Yoo claim that by 2023 worldwide spending on drones will increase by what factor?

2. According to the authors, which two countries secretly flouted the Washington Naval Treaty of 1922?

3. According to Herman and Yoo, what saved Great Britain from Nazi Germany's air forces during World War II?

The most important military revolution of our time, the development of unmanned aerial vehicles (UAVs), is well under way. In 2000, our military had 60 UAVs. Today it has at least 6,000, with more to come. From the Hellfire-missile-carrying Predator to the Global Hawk with its wingspan of 130 feet to the tiny Raven, which carries a camera the size of a peanut, UAVs are becoming ubiquitous, and drone strikes increasingly precise. Many people wonder where this technology is heading—and whether we need new laws and international agreements to keep the drone revolution from flying out of control.

Former *New York Times* editor Bill Keller has proclaimed that drones are "propelling us to the day when we cede . . . lethal authority to software," while legal scholars question whether death by drone might violate international law. Radford University philosophy and peace-studies professor Glen T. Martin has written that this technology is "attacking the heart of civilization itself," while two authors recently opined in the *Wall Street Journal* that, thanks to drones, "the West risks, however inadvertently, going down the same path" as the one that led to Auschwitz. These fears are misplaced and overstated. History shows that the best safeguards against the abuse of new technologies are new technologies themselves.

China, the Europeans, and the Russians are all anxious to build their own UAV fleets and make up for time lost to the United States and Israel. Worldwide spending on drones is expected to double by 2023. As innovation in UAVs and similar devices accelerates, it will be more important than ever that the United States maintain its current edge.

General Atomics, creator of the now notorious Predator, is already replacing it with the MQ-9 Reaper, which has three times the cruising speed and carries 15 times the deadly ordnance. The Russians are building their own counterpart to the Reaper, which is expected to be in production by 2016.

Today's Predator will look like a World War I Sopwith Camel compared with the UAVs that military researchers will unveil in just a decade or two. Boeing is currently at work on an unmanned glider—called the Phantom Eye—with half a football field's worth of wingspan and powered by solar energy and liquid hydrogen that will keep it aloft for four days at a time (today's Global Hawk can manage 35 hours). The Defense Advanced Research Projects Agency has been designing drones that will be able to stay on mission for five years without returning to Earth.

The most sophisticated unmanned systems will fly at supersonic speed and employ stealth technology and miniaturization. Northrop Grumman's X-47 unmanned stealth bomber lands by itself on aircraft carriers and is already in prototype. Drones that fit in the palm of the hand and can fly like a bird and hover like an insect are already in use, for example TechJect's Dragonfly, a UAV developed for the Air Force and available for purchase at $119 apiece. Lockheed Martin is working on a drone the size of a maple-tree seed that can perch and look into windows, climb walls or pipes, and insert a poisonous syringe into an unsuspecting target.

Meanwhile, the development of unmanned underwater vehicles (UUVs) is also proceeding, from surveillance surface craft able to detect mines and protect naval installations to miniature unmanned submarines and underwater attack craft. Unmanned seacraft that mimic the swimming motion of fish have been under development for a decade; the Office of Naval Research has a project for creating robotic jellyfish that can drift unseen with sea currents and attach themselves to an enemy vessel or installation before detonating. Before the decade is out, the UUV revolution is going to cause almost as many headaches for maritime lawyers as the UAV revolution already has for experts on the laws of war.

So are we about to enter a killer-drone nightmare, in which only international agreements and control can stop a global Terminator-style Armageddon?

Sadly, the historical record of international agreements in keeping the peace and limiting carnage is weak. A close examination of efforts to control new technologies suggests that deterrence through technological progress is more likely to prevent misuse of UAVs.

National leaders and international lawyers have often responded to innovations in the field of arms with efforts at regulation. Most of these efforts have simply failed. Take, for example, the emergence of air power. After the Wright brothers launched the first airplane at Kitty Hawk, nations began to develop rudimentary military aircraft. The Wright brothers themselves established what eventually became known as the Curtiss-Wright company, which produced the World War II P-40 fighter, among other aircraft. Air power's first real test came in the Great War, when Allied and German planes not only undertook reconnaissance missions but dropped the first aerial bombs and fought one another in the skies. Some international lawyers argued at the time that air strikes against ground targets were illegal because the pilots fought at a distance without putting themselves at personal risk (an early version of one of the current arguments against drones). But the nations at war kept pressing for the development of weapons in the air, and restraints on the destructiveness of aircraft came from new anti-aircraft weapons and fighter planes.

International lawyers next argued that air attacks must not target population centers, but the Spanish Civil War and then the German, British, and American bombing runs on European and Japanese cities displayed the futility of attempting to outlaw such strikes. International treaties on the laws of war today prohibit directly targeting civilians, but the United States and its allies will continue to launch attacks on military targets that cause civilian collateral damage and even hit non-military targets (such as office buildings and electrical plants) that support a regime.

A similar story played out with submarines. In World War I, submarines gave the German Empire a new weapon with which to combat the Allied blockade and to enforce a blockade of its own. The Allies sought to neutralize this innovation by claiming that international law required submarines to surface and provide civilians a chance to escape before sinking their vessels. Submarines, however, were not defeated by international law, but by the convoy strategy and new methods for detecting and attacking undersea craft. And once the Allies had developed their own submarines, they showed no commitment to their claims about international law. When World War II came, the United States Navy used submarines to great effect, virtually wiping out Japan's merchant marine and handicapping its navy. Advances in technology, rather than treaties, have limited the scope of submarine warfare.

Efforts to restrain the advance of military technology have sometimes disadvantaged democracies, which tend to observe treaties more faithfully than authoritarian nations do. After World War I, the great powers entered into the Washington Naval Treaty of 1922 to forestall competition in building up naval fleets. The treaty sought to freeze the sizes of the fleets of Great Britain, the United States, France, Germany, and Japan and to prevent the development of larger ships and better armaments. While the democracies obeyed the agreement, Germany and Japan cheated by secretly developing new and larger battleships. The treaty restrictions also encouraged Japan to develop aircraft carriers and naval aviation, which were not covered by the agreement, while Britain and the U.S. slept.

When restraint in arms buildups has occurred, it has come primarily from deterrence. Chemical weapons were another of

The Need for Armed Drones

The debate within the international legal, academic, and human rights communities on the legality and propriety of drone strikes will likely continue unabated. To surrender to the demands of such critics would be equivalent to forgetting the lessons of September 11 [referring to the 2001 terrorist attacks on the United States], when a small, non-state terrorist organization operating from a nation with which the United States was not at war planned and launched an attack that killed almost 3,000 Americans.

The United States should preserve its ability to use all of the tools in its arsenal to ensure that the plots hatched by terrorist organizations do not become successful attacks on the U.S. homeland. Armed drones have proved to be one of the most effective and discriminating tools available to U.S. forces, and their lawful use should continue until such time as non-state, transnational terrorist organizations no longer present an imminent threat to the United States.

Steven Groves, "Drone Strikes:
The Legality of U.S. Targeting Terrorists Abroad,"
Heritage Foundation Backgrounder, no. 2788,
April 9, 2013.

World War I's horrifying innovations. They inflicted a level of suffering and terror that could not be strategically justified. But during the interwar years, the great powers failed to reach any agreement to limit their use in combat—the Chemical Weapons Convention would not come into existence until the 1990s. Nevertheless, the Axis and Allied powers did not resort to chemical weapons in a war of ideologies that caused more death and destruction than had the preceding world war.

Why? Historical research has shown that [Adolf] Hitler's Germany never deployed its chemical weapons arsenal because it knew that the Allies would respond in kind. The same went for the superpowers' nuclear arsenals during the Cold War. Treaties did not stop the development of fission and then fusion weapons, strategic bombers, and intercontinental ballistic missiles. Only the competition of the U.S. and the USSR [Soviet Union] to match each other's stockpiles prevented a nuclear exchange.

While the politicians, lawyers, and bureaucrats debate and dither, the rate of technological advance increases. The record of deterrence and counter-technologies in limiting the destructive potential of new technologies is strong. Rather than try to stop development with parchment barriers that hinder us more than our enemies, we should recognize that UAV technology itself may help us achieve the fundamental goal of the laws of war: to spare civilians and to reduce death and destruction on the battlefield.

Virtually all technological evolution in UAVs makes them not only more stealthy but also more precise—which means less loss of innocent life and less unintended physical destruction. Far from making war less civilized, drones are part of a trend toward "smart" weapons that has steadily made warfare less indiscriminate over the past half century. This trend will continue. Instead of blowing up a carful of people in order to take out an identified terrorist, as today's Predator does, a device like Lockheed Martin's maple-seed-sized drone will be able to detect and kill that single passenger, leaving the rest unharmed.

What about the danger that fully automated systems might take the decision to kill away from human beings and leave it to the robots themselves? As Werner Dahm, former chief scientist of the Air Force, wrote in the *Wall Street Journal*, we should "expect to see humans 'in the loop' for a long, long time to come." This is because deciding when actually to kill a target is the simplest link in a UAV's so-called kill-chain sequence—much simpler than detecting a target and delivering the lethal ordnance accurately and on time once the kill decision has been made. The military doesn't want fully automated systems because, as Dahm notes, "we don't gain anything" from them if they work—and there's plenty of pain if they don't. Even so, Georgia Institute of Technology's Ronald Arkin predicts that future technology will be able to give us robot soldiers that perform more "ethically than human soldiers are capable of," since they'll perform on the battlefield without anger or a desire to punish or take revenge.

On the other hand, a truly inhumane robot weapon—one designed to cause the most collateral damage and whose devastating psychological impact on a civilian population is enhanced by remote automatic detonation—is precisely what our military is least likely to create but a rogue nation or terrorist group is most likely to want and develop. Protection from that kind of attack can come only through a superior knowledge of drone technologies—from knowing how to detect and shoot them down to having the ability to hack and electronically jam them.

It wasn't treaties or agreements that protected Britain from Hitler's Luftwaffe in 1940, it was the Spitfire fighter—and something similar will be true in the brave new world of UAVs.

Periodical and Internet Sources Bibliography

The following articles have been selected to supplement the diverse views presented in this chapter.

Peter Beinart	"Hillary Clinton's Bizarre Critique of U.S. Foreign Policy," *Atlantic*, July 17, 2014.
Stephen Blank	"The Dumbing-Down of Foreign Policy," *U.S. News & World Report*, November 19, 2013.
Mark Bowden	"The Killing Machines: How to Think About Drones," *Atlantic*, August 14, 2013.
Michael A. Cohen	"Americans Are Incoherent on Foreign Policy," *Boston Globe*, September 20, 2014.
Josh Gerstein	"Obama's Blurry Foreign Policy Vision," *Politico*, August 27, 2014.
Michael Hastings	"The Rise of the Killer Drones: How America Goes to War in Secret," *Rolling Stone*, April 26, 2012.
Josh Hicks	"Both Parties Criticize Obama Foreign Policy," *Pittsburgh Post-Gazette*, September 1, 2014.
Kim R. Holmes and William Inboden	"The U.S. Needs a New Foreign Policy Agenda for 2016 (Part Two of Four)," *Foreign Policy*, September 23 2014.
Elise Labott, Richard Roth, and Josh Levs	"Has Gaza Conflict Brought New Low in U.S.-Israel Relationship?," CNN, August 5, 2014.
David Pilling	"Legal or Not, Drone Strikes Set a Dangerous Precedent," *Financial Times*, October 23, 2013.
Kristin Roberts	"When the Whole World Has Drones," *National Journal*, March 21, 2013.

OPPOSING
VIEWPOINTS®
SERIES

CHAPTER 2

Are Foreign Military Interventions Good for the United States?

Chapter Preface

The most significant military interventions by the United States in the twenty-first century were the wars in Afghanistan and Iraq. These interventions caused controversy both domestically and internationally. At the present time, American public opinion of US military involvement abroad has become less enthusiastic, but this has not always been the case.

American opinion about the war in Afghanistan was quite different at the start of the war than it is currently. A Gallup poll taken in October 2001, at the start of the war in Afghanistan, found that 82 percent of Americans favored US military actions in Afghanistan, with only 14 percent opposing such involvement. Gallup took a survey in February 2014, asking, "Looking back, do you think the United States made a mistake sending troops to fight in Afghanistan in 2001?" In this poll, 49 percent of Americans said that the United States did make a mistake in sending troops to Afghanistan, whereas 48 percent said that it was not a mistake. A Pew Research Center/ *USA Today* poll from January 2014 found that more than half of Americans believed that the United States mostly failed in achieving its goals in Afghanistan.

Similarly, American opinion about the war in Iraq has grown more negative over time. A Gallup poll taken in February 2003, at the start of the war in Iraq, showed that 59 percent of Americans favored military actions in Iraq, with 37 percent opposing. However, a Pew Research Center/*USA Today* poll from January 2014 found that 50 percent of Americans polled believed that the decision to use military force in Iraq was the wrong decision, whereas only 38 percent thought it was the right decision. In addition, 52 percent said that the United States failed in achieving its goals in Iraq. A CBS News poll in December 2013 found that 49 percent of Americans said removing Saddam Hussein from power was not worth the loss of American lives and other costs of attacking Iraq, whereas only 36 percent said it was worth it.

A 2010 Pew Research Center's Global Attitudes Project survey found that the majority of people in twenty-two different countries surveyed around the world do not approve of President Barack Obama's handling of the wars in Afghanistan or Iraq, especially in countries of the Middle East, Asia, and South America. The criticism of US military involvement domestically and internationally possibly explains President Obama's decision in 2013 to not take military action against Syria. In September 2013, a Gallup poll showed that more than half of Americans opposed US military action in Syria, even knowing that Syrian president Bashar al-Assad had used chemical weapons against his own people. Public opinion about US military involvement is not the only factor taken into consideration, but negative public opinion no doubt also makes any particular military invasion less likely.

The following chapter examines US military intervention abroad and debates the outcomes of the wars in Iraq and Afghanistan, as well as the outcome of the president's decision in 2013 not to launch a military offensive in Syria.

| "American combat operations in Iraq
did a great good."

The United States Achieved Major Accomplishments in the Iraq War

Ben Voth

In the following viewpoint, Ben Voth argues that despite a negative view of the war in Iraq by the antiwar movement, the United States had four major accomplishments from the war. Voth claims that American military operations benefitted Iraq and the world by removing Saddam Hussein from power, restoring respect for American military power, creating a defense against al Qaeda in the Middle East, and demonstrating the possibility of democracy in that region. Voth is chair of corporate communications and public affairs at Southern Methodist University in Dallas, Texas.

As you read, consider the following questions:

1. According to Voth, how many Kurds did Saddam Hussein kill under a policy of genocide?

2. According to the author, what percentage of Iraqis disapprove of al Qaeda?

3. According to Voth, which of Iraq's neighbors has been inspired by Iraq's growing democracy and openness?

The United States has concluded major combat operations in Iraq. After seven years of war, it is important to remember the good accomplished by these efforts. The rhetorical interpretation of the war in many respects overwhelmed the facts on the ground. For the first five years of combat operations, a tremendous global effort was directed by our educated elite to mislead the public about the good accomplished among the 27 million human beings trapped in the inhumane spectacle of Saddam Hussein's governance. Several major accomplishments should be recorded in the midst of this vast misinformation regime that unfortunately seeks to lodge morality in the selective, myopic vision of the antiwar movement.

1. Removing from political power one of the world's most notorious genocidaires: Saddam Hussein.

Saddam Hussein conducted the deadliest war (the Iran-Iraq War) since World War II, killing more than a million people. The war killed tens of thousands of teenage boys and hundreds of thousands of civilians. Saddam Hussein created some of the world's largest ecological disasters, including the massive gulf oil spill that exponentially dwarfs other fodder for alarmists such as the BP Gulf [of Mexico] spill. Saddam Hussein conducted genocidal policies against ethnic minorities such as the Kurds of northern Iraq. He distinguished himself by using weapons of mass destruction on women and children at Halabja. These were among the more than 300,000 Kurds he killed in an internationally ignored policy of genocide.

The details of his brutal reign were vividly accounted for in 2002 by noted genocide author (and [President Barack] Obama advisor) Samantha Power. Her account of global genocide severely chastised the global ambivalence to this usage of weapons of mass destruction against civilians. The bipartisan

U.S. congressional authorization for force against Saddam Hussein repeatedly referenced these humanitarian violations rooted in this obscene usage of chemical weapons. Saddam Hussein was finally removed from power in 2003, put on trial in Iraq by Iraqis, and put to death by Iraqis for his crimes against Iraqi civilians. His removal brought an end to these various genocidal policies and has rendered northern Iraq one of the nation's most supportive regions with regard to the American military operations that so profoundly benefited their daily livelihoods.

2. Restoring the viability of American military power as a global tool.

Osama bin Laden rightly described the United States in the 1990s as a global "paper tiger" unwilling to risk more than the few men lost in Mogadishu [capital of Somalia]. He was, at that point, empirically correct. He suggested to Muslim listeners that they should prefer the "strong horse" of al-Qaeda, which would eagerly sacrifice so many more lives for bin Laden's hideous agenda. After thousands of American combat deaths and a vicious propaganda war against American military might, not only did the American force in Iraq refuse to withdraw, but in 2007, the force was escalated in what has become the new American model for responding to insurgencies.

Prior to Iraq, rivals to American power knew that mere dozens of American soldiers needed to be killed in order to ignite the allegedly moral antiwar movement to tip America's public sphere toward withdrawal. Such withdrawals would then allow for ensuing genocide and eliminationism, as seen in places such as Cambodia. That rhetorical order now lies shattered at the feet of an American president "surging" in Afghanistan and who said in his speech accepting a Nobel Peace Prize that war does solve problems. As a result, global tyrants do not have a currently reliable calculus for continuing with their inhumane practices.

President Barack Obama on War

We must begin by acknowledging the hard truth: We will not eradicate violent conflict in our lifetimes. There will be times when nations—acting individually or in concert—will find the use of force not only necessary but morally justified.

I make this statement mindful of what Martin Luther King Jr. said in this same ceremony years ago: "Violence never brings permanent peace. It solves no social problem: It merely creates new and more complicated ones." As someone who stands here as a direct consequence of Dr. King's life work, I am living testimony to the moral force of nonviolence. I know there's nothing weak—nothing passive—nothing naïve—in the creed and lives of Gandhi and King.

But as a head of state sworn to protect and defend my nation, I cannot be guided by their examples alone. I face the world as it is, and cannot stand idle in the face of threats to the American people. For make no mistake: Evil does exist in the world. A nonviolent movement could not have halted [Adolf] Hitler's armies. Negotiations cannot convince al Qaeda's leaders to lay down their arms. To say that force may sometimes be necessary is not a call to cynicism—it is a recognition of history; the imperfections of man and the limits of reason.

Barack H. Obama, Nobel Lecture, December 10, 2009.

3. Building a bulwark in the Middle East against al-Qaeda.

Al-Qaeda and Shia radicals have engineered a public relations disaster of mammoth proportions within the nation-state of Iraq. Iraqis "hate" al-Qaeda. Public opinion polls of Iraqis show that more than 90% of Iraqis disapprove of al-

Qaeda. More than 80% strongly disapprove. The brutal daily regimen of slaughtering mothers, fathers, brothers, sisters, infants, children, and the disabled—the preponderance of victims being Muslim—has enraged the Iraqi consciousness. The bombings of marketplaces, mosques, police stations, schools and any other locale of civilian gatherings has left an unbleachable stain on the rhetorical brand of al-Qaeda. Iraqis are not the fools that antiwar paternalists have taken them to be. Iraqis see who dress in uniform to distinguish themselves from civilians, and they see who dress as women to walk into civilian centers and author their "deaths as texts" with help from the blood of innocents. There will likely be no more enduring public on the question of squashing and removing the viral consciousness of al-Qaeda from the global public sphere. The Iraqis will be stalwarts on the vivid question of terrorism as a political tool.

4. Demonstrating the viability of democracy in the Middle East.

By 2005, Iraq was able to conduct three national elections and adopt a constitution. This happened while the constitution of the European Union failed to pass. Naysayers said the Iraqis would not be able to secure election sites to carry off any of these democratic functions. However, they carried off three such events, and all of them were better attended than any recent American election. Despite vile attacks on polling centers (that in one instance loaded a disabled man full of explosives into a van carrying voters), the experiment in democracy proceeded with enthusiasm. The purple fingers of Iraqis [purple indicates the ink stain on the index fingers of first-time voters in the 2005 Iraqi election] were brandished with pride alongside bright smiles.

The optimistic defiance was a sharp, inspiring contrast to the blood-soaked streets sought by the rejectionists. The democracy has notable regional effects. Kuwait, which had its democracy propelled after the first invasion of Iraq, recently witnessed the surprising rise of female political candidates to office. The right of women to vote is years later bearing the fruit of women in power. Iran's totalitarianism has been internally racked by the green movement inspired by greater expectations of democracy and openness patent in their Iraqi neighbor.

[President Abraham] Lincoln rightly observed at Gettysburg the importance of realizing that these soldiers have not died in vain. This American idealism still rings true today. The more than four thousand American lives given as our most precious expenditure should be remembered for the good they did—not for themselves, not for their nation, not for the people of Iraq, but for the entire human family that has suffered too many Saddam Husseins and too much public ambivalence falsely portrayed as proper moral restraint. American combat operations in Iraq did a great good, and we would do well to forever observe these great facts and so many more.

"In the midst of an invasion into one far-flung land with a clear directive, talk turned to conquering another with a premise as preposterous as it was dangerous."

The United States Has Suffered Many Consequences from the Iraq War

Jamie Tarabay

In the following viewpoint, Jamie Tarabay argues that despite continued claims of success in the war in Iraq, the real costs of the war include both economic and international opportunity costs. Tarabay contends that the Iraq War has led to several negative consequences, including displaced Iraqis, an emboldened Iran, and an arrogant new prime minister. Tarabay also claims there is no reason to believe that the war led to the Arab Spring, a series of antigovernment uprisings in the Arab world beginning in 2010. Tarabay is a senior staff writer at Al Jazeera America.

As you read, consider the following questions:

1. According to Tarabay, when did talk of invading Iraq begin?

2. What two examples does the author give of breaches of American military protocol that occurred during the Iraq War?

3. The author compares the prime minister of Iraq, Nouri al-Maliki, to whom?

When people talk about the cost of the war in Iraq, they speak about the hundreds of billions of dollars that frittered away in the Mesopotamian dust and the spilled blood of Iraqi, American, British, Italian, Polish, Spanish and countless other souls swept up in a conflict that has no natural ending.

The Costs of the Iraq War

They talk about the domestic opportunity cost and just what those hundreds of billions of dollars could have bought at home instead of the military hardware that began falling apart less than two years after the invasion began, or idealistic infrastructure projects all over Iraq that deteriorated in a pit of corruption and neglect.

They talk about the advancements in education, health care and a national transportation system that could have been funded instead, or the possibility that the global financial crisis might not have hit the U.S. economy quite so hard had that money not been spent on a war at a time of the U.S.'s choosing.

While all those costs should be taken into consideration, another looms just as large: the international opportunity cost.

The Justification for the Iraq War

When the White House of [President] George W. Bush and [Vice President] Dick Cheney began beating the drums for an invasion of Iraq in 2002, the rest of the world was still digesting the horror of the September 11, 2001, attacks and the subsequent war in Afghanistan. If there ever was a coalition of the willing, it was there, diplomatically and militarily, ready to hit at a threat that most Western countries, at least, perceived as a global threat.

Yet in the midst of an invasion into one far-flung land with a clear directive, talk turned to conquering another with a premise as preposterous as it was dangerous. The threat of weapons of mass destruction [WMD], missiles 45 minutes from being launched at British targets in the Mediterranean, and the biggest doozy of them all: operational collaboration and actual links between Saddam Hussein and al-Qaida.

There was as much connection between Saddam Hussein and al-Qaida as there is between eating bread crusts and having curly hair. Even as CIA [Central Intelligence Agency] intelligence told them otherwise, White House officials and other neoconservatives pounded the claim . . . until it was eventually debunked years later in declassified documents.

The support from the rest of the world dropped off. The U.S. had to tout lists of countries willing to be publicly associated with any action in Iraq. It didn't include Arab nations. It was not clear where—and with whom—Bush's "with us or against us" policy might end.

Once the search for WMD turned up empty-handed, the administration began recalibrating its reasons for being there. It went from declaring the fall of a tyrant and the establishment of a real Arab democracy in the Middle East, to creating enough of a stable security environment to allow Iraq's splintered politicians to seal their own vacuum.

The Consequences of the Iraq War

Finally, ten years on, a global consideration of the war in Iraq reveals these consequences:

- More than a million Iraqi refugees scattered across the world in countries that will accept them.

- More than three million Iraqis displaced within the country, pushed out of their homes and running from sectarian violence.

- A rupture in diplomatic and security alliances across the Middle East that has irrevocably altered the landscape for U.S. and Western strategic interests.

- A rising Iran, emboldened by the death of its main nemesis, now exerts greater influence over a region stretching from the Persian sands all the way to the verdant Levant.

- A loss of face for the U.S. in the Middle East and North Africa and a dent in its image as a military superpower after being undercut and hammered for years by militia groups in the streets of Baghdad, Diyala and Ramadi.

- The Abu Ghraib prisoner abuse scandal, the Haditha massacre and other breaches of American military protocol paralyzed the administration's efforts to 'win hearts and minds' in Iraq and set back by years efforts to stabilize the region.

- A war in Afghanistan that has dragged on for years longer than it ever should have, its initial aim of taking Osama bin Laden decimated after the al-Qaida leader was found and killed in Pakistan. The cost of the U.S. military presence now (combined with Iraq) tops a trillion dollars, and a resurgent Taliban is threatening to retake power in many places the U.S. failed to win over before the majority of its forces finally leave next year [in 2014].

Yet there continues to be talk of success by unrepentant former officials and hawks then bent on war, now touting memoirs, even as the real cost comes home—in the thousands of American lives lost and the families they've left behind, in the wider legacy of the hundreds of thousands of servicemen and women who suffer from ailments ranging from post-traumatic stress [disorder] or traumatic brain injury, to the loss of a limb, an eye, or burns.

The New Iraqi Government

It is also worth noting that U.S. and other oil companies around the world are finding resistance from Iraq to privatize its oil sector and are balking at the severe conditions the Iraqi government is placing on any contracts with foreign oil companies.

At the heart of the idea of any possible U.S. influence in Iraq sits a man whose behavior more closely identifies with his dictatorial predecessor than a democratic aspirant, a man who has made it his mission to demonstrate that no state, be it the U.S. or Iran, can tell him what to do. In his brilliant portrait of Nouri al-Maliki, longtime foreign correspondent Ned Parker details how Iraq's current prime minister solidified his hold on power through unsavory political alliances, creating a new security command that answered solely to him, bullying his adversaries, and arresting those who resisted. Parker writes that Maliki, who has also expressed his support for besieged Syrian president Bashar al-Assad, could serve as a lesson for other Islamist leaders in the region attempting to govern in a new world.

"It is arrogant to think the West can shape Iraq's destiny or Maliki's behavior, but neither does the United States have to enable Iraq's slow downward spiral," Parker writes. "At this point, the United States has likely ceded most of its influence in Iraq through inertia and lack of vision, but the fading relationship still provides an opening to encourage the country's

The Monetary Cost of the Wars in Afghanistan and Iraq

By the most conservative reckoning, the Iraq and Afghanistan conflicts will cost $4 trillion, including operations to date, accrued veterans' medical and disability costs; indirect costs to the Defense Department, social costs for veterans' families and interest already paid. Any estimation of macroeconomic costs, such as the impact of higher oil prices on weakening aggregate demand, and the link between oil prices and decisions of the Federal Reserve to loosen monetary and regulatory policy prior to the financial crisis, would easily raise the cost to $5 or $6 trillion, (even if only a fraction of the "blame" is attributed to the wars). Throughout the past decade, the United States has underestimated the length, difficulty, cost and economic consequences of these wars and has failed to plan how to pay for them.

What did we buy for $4 trillion? The U.S. still faces a perilous international security situation and a fragile economy. Today as the country considers how to improve its balance sheet, it could have been hoped that the ending of the wars would provide a peace dividend, such as the one during the [Bill] Clinton administration that helped Americans to invest more in butter and less in guns.

Linda J. Bilmes,
"The Financial Legacy of Iraq and Afghanistan:
How Wartime Spending Decisions Will Constrain
Future National Security Budgets," Harvard Kennedy School
Faculty Research Working Paper Series RWP13-006,
March 2013.

leaders to turn away from their darker impulses and pursue genuine institution building. The alternative risks the demise of the Iraqi state and years of bloody civil war."

The Iraq War and the Arab Spring

It is also worth noting the utter falsity of the claim from those who'd supported the invasion into Iraq that the demise of Saddam Hussein led, in part, to the Arab Spring [a series of antigovernment uprisings affecting the Arab world beginning in 2010]. Both former Secretary of State Condoleezza Rice and Vice President Cheney credit American actions in Iraq as having a role in unseating some of the region's most immoveable autocrats.

There is no evidence to suggest that a burgeoning Shiite revival in Iraq would have influenced Mohamed Bouazizi to set himself on fire in front of the municipal headquarters of Sidi Bouzid, a small town south of Tunis [the capital of Tunisia]. More likely, as Egyptians, Libyans, Moroccans and other Tunisians have themselves so fluently expressed, their motivation was missed opportunities, economic or otherwise.

The better question to ask is: Had there been no invasion into Iraq, might the Arab Spring have extended into Saddam's Iraq? Might it not have fuelled a Shiite uprising there, where, perhaps, the U.S. administration and other allies might send aid in the form of no-fly zones, or even weapons to friendly rebels in the south and the north? The Iraqis would have then perhaps been able to form their own Islamist government, likely similar to the one it has now, and contend with the sectarian issues it faces today without recoiling at American overtures for support.

That is one thing we will never know, and the cost of that is immeasurable.

"The war in Afghanistan is not yet lost. We are not yet losing, in fact, and success remains possible."

The War in Afghanistan Has Made Progress and Should Continue

Frederick W. Kagan and Kimberly Kagan

In the following viewpoint, Frederick W. Kagan and Kimberly Kagan argue that American troops should remain in Afghanistan in order to win the war. The authors contend that the plans to withdraw a significant number of troops are premature and that the president should reconsider removing military forces when success remains possible. Frederick W. Kagan is an American resident scholar at the American Enterprise Institute, and Kimberly Kagan is the founder and president of the Institute for the Study of War.

As you read, consider the following questions:

1. According to the authors, how many troops were to be withdrawn between November 2013 and February 2014?

2. The authors contend that it is important for the United States to support the current force of how many Afghan National Security Forces (ANSF) through 2017?

3. What do the authors say about the cost of keeping thirty-four thousand troops in Afghanistan for another six or eight months?

President [Barack] Obama's decision to withdraw another 34,000 troops from Afghanistan over the course of the next year is unwise. It greatly increases the risk of mission failure in that important conflict, jeopardizing gains already made in the Taliban heartland in the south and compromising the ability of Afghan and coalition forces to finish the fight against the Haqqani network in the east. It also increases the risk that al Qaeda will be able to reestablish itself in limited safe havens in Afghanistan over time. Removing troops and capabilities before Afghanistan's next presidential election, scheduled for April 2014, further exacerbates the danger that Afghanistan might collapse into renewed ethnic civil war.

The Drawdown of American Troops in Afghanistan

It was not as bad as it might have been, however, and prospects for success in this conflict remain, although the odds grow ever longer. The president appears to have yielded to military realities and the laws of physics on a number of important points. The drawdown itself is paced to keep a significant number of American troops in Afghanistan through most of this coming fighting season: Around 6,000 troops are to be withdrawn between now and this spring; another 8,000 by November; and the final 20,000 by February 2014.

Senior administration officials explained on background that the first stage of this withdrawal is already under way and results largely from the deployment of brigades configured to conduct training and advising missions rather than combat.

General Joe Dunford, the new commander in Afghanistan, will therefore have to redeploy only another 8,000 troops while fighting the enemy this summer—a far more manageable challenge than if he had had to redeploy the full 28,000 while still trying to accomplish his primary mission of helping the Afghans defeat our common enemies and consolidate gains. Administration officials also said that a sizable contingent of planners and logisticians now in Afghanistan to design and execute the drawdown are not counted against the total troop numbers—a vital fact, since writing and implementing such a plan is a massive undertaking that could well otherwise consume the staffs and commanders who must focus on continuing progress against the enemy and training the Afghan National Security Forces (ANSF).

The president has also postponed an announcement—and, according to administration officials, even the decision—on the size of the post-2014 U.S. military presence in Afghanistan. That postponement is very wise. The discussion of the long-term presence is premature at this stage of the campaign. It is impossible to describe the security situation in 2015 before the 2013 fighting season has even begun. And considering that administration officials were floating the idea of keeping no troops at all in Afghanistan after 2014 when President Hamid Karzai came to Washington in January, the deferral of a decision on this matter is a relief.

Perhaps the most encouraging part of the change in the White House decision making is that—according to senior administration briefers—plans to cut the ANSF by more than 100,000 troops starting in 2015 are not final. It appears that the president is considering supporting the current force of 352,000 ANSF troops through 2017 instead. Maintaining a large ANSF is absolutely vital. It is almost impossible to imagine a security situation in 2015 in which dismissing more than 100,000 trained Afghan soldiers and police (meaning unemployment for many of them) makes any sense. It is equally

President Barack Obama on the War in Afghanistan

When I took office, nearly 180,000 Americans were serving in Iraq and Afghanistan. Today, all our troops are out of Iraq. More than 60,000 of our troops have already come home from Afghanistan. With Afghan forces now in the lead for their own security, our troops have moved to a support role. Together with our allies, we will complete our mission there by the end of this year [2014], and America's longest war will finally be over.

After 2014, we will support a unified Afghanistan as it takes responsibility for its own future. If the Afghan government signs a security agreement that we have negotiated, a small force of Americans could remain in Afghanistan with NATO [North Atlantic Treaty Organization] allies to carry out two narrow missions: training and assisting Afghan forces, and counterterrorism operations to pursue any remnants of al Qaeda. For while our relationship with Afghanistan will change, one thing will not: our resolve that terrorists do not launch attacks against our country.

The fact is, that danger remains. While we have put al Qaeda's core leadership on a path to defeat, the threat has evolved, as al Qaeda affiliates and other extremists take root in different parts of the world.

President Barack Obama,
State of the Union Address,
January 28, 2014.

important to wait until we have seen how Afghan forces perform after the American and international mission changes in 2015 before deciding on the future size and composition of those forces.

The Possibility of Success in Afghanistan

It is still possible, therefore, that coalition and Afghan troops may be able to hold on to gains already made and even expand them over the course of this fighting season. That hope justifies continued support for an important mission, as well as continued pressure on the White House to reduce the enormous risks it is assuming in Afghanistan in pursuit of extremely small rhetorical, political, and economic benefits.

The cost of keeping 14,000 troops in Afghanistan until next February rather than bringing them out by November is budget dust in the context of overall defense spending, let alone the national debt, the deficit, or any major social program. Even the cost of keeping all 34,000 troops now scheduled to come out over the next year in Afghanistan for another six or eight months would hardly register compared with other budget items. Administration officials accurately and honestly insisted that withdrawing those forces increases the risk of failure in Afghanistan. Accepting that increased risk—on top of the enormous risks the administration has already accepted by previous premature troop withdrawal—is difficult to justify.

The president's decision on Afghanistan was not as bad as it might have been—indeed, it was not as bad as it seemed certain to be at the start of this year. It leaves a glimmer of hope for success, which our commanders, troops, and diplomats in the field will exert all their powers to keep alive. But it was still a mistake that puts our nation's security in greater jeopardy. We hope that the president will continue to reevaluate his own willingness to accept risk in light of the rapidly diminishing economic and political returns he will receive from lowering force levels.

The war in Afghanistan is not yet lost. We are not yet losing, in fact, and success remains possible. But it is absolutely vital that the White House give General Dunford some flexibility to adjust the withdrawal timelines, and even to ask for temporary reinforcements, as the situation on the ground evolves.

> "With the exception of the current U.S. commander in Afghanistan, virtually everyone has concluded that the war has been a disaster for all involved."

Afghanistan: Is It Really the End Game?

Conn Hallinan

In the following viewpoint, Conn Hallinan argues that the war in Afghanistan has been a failure and that the United States should end the military intervention there immediately. Hallinan claims that the war has caused many casualties without any real negotiations to end the fighting. Hallinan contends that a real solution will have to involve negotiations with the Taliban, which is something the United States has been unwilling to support. Hallinan is a columnist for Foreign Policy in Focus, a project of the Institute for Policy Studies.

As you read, consider the following questions:

1. According to Hallinan, how many Afghans have been killed in the wars of the last thirty years?

2. What American presence will remain in Afghanistan until 2024, according to the author?

3. The author claims that the Taliban itself and a recent Asia Foundation poll found that what percentage of Afghans support the Taliban?

There is nothing that better sums up the utter failure of America's longest war than international forces getting ambushed as they try to get the hell out of the county. And yet the April 1 [2013] debacle in Baluchistan was in many ways a metaphor for a looming crisis that NATO and the United States seem totally unprepared for: with the clock ticking down on removing most combat troops by 2014, there are no official negotiations going on, nor does there seem to be any strategy for how to bring them about.

"I still cannot understand how we, the international community and the Afghan government have managed to arrive at a situation in which everything is coming together in 2014—elections, new president, economic transition, military transition—and negotiations for the peace process have not really started," as Bernard Bajolet, the former French ambassador to Kabul and current head of France's foreign intelligence service, told the *New York Times*.

When the Obama administration sent an additional 30,000 troops into Afghanistan in 2009 as part of the "surge," the goal was to secure the country's southern provinces, suppress opium cultivation, and force the Taliban to give up on the war. Not only did the surge fail to impress the Taliban and its allies, it never stabilized the southern provinces of Helmand and Kandahar. Both are once again under the sway of the insurgency, and opium production has soared. What the surge did manage was to spread the insurgency into formerly secure areas in the north and west.

With the exception of the current U.S. commander in Afghanistan, virtually everyone has concluded that the war has been a disaster for all involved.

"Shoot and Talk"

Afghanistan has lost more than 2 million people to the wars of the past 30 years. Huge sections of the population have been turned into refugees, and the country is becoming what one international law enforcement official described to the *New York Times* as "the world's first true narco state." According to the World Bank, 36 percent of Afghans are at or below the poverty line, and 20 percent of Afghan children never reach the age of five.

The war has cost American taxpayers over $1.4 trillion, and according to a recent study, the final butcher bill for Iraq and Afghanistan together will top $6 trillion. The decade-long conflict has put enormous strains on the NATO alliance, destabilized and alienated nuclear-armed Pakistan, and helped to spread al-Qaeda-like organizations throughout the Middle East and Africa.

Only U.S. Gen. Joseph "Fighting Joe" Dunford, head of the International Security Assistance Force (ISAF) thinks the war on the Taliban is being won, and that the Afghan army is "steadily gaining in confidence, competence, and commitment." Attacks by the Taliban are up 47 percent over last year, and the casualty rate for Afghan soldiers and police has increased 40 percent. The yearly desertion rate of the Afghan army is between 27 percent and 30 percent.

In theory, ISAF combat troops will exit Afghanistan in 2014 and turn the war over to the Afghan army and police, organizations that have yet to show they can take on the insurgency. One of the army's crack units was recently overrun in eastern Afghanistan. Given the fragility of the Afghan government and its army, one would think that the White House would be putting on a full-court press to get talks going, but instead it is following a strategy that has demonstrably failed in the past.

The tactic of "shooting and talking," central to the surge, has produced lots of casualties but virtually zero dialogue—hardly a surprise. That approach has never worked in Afghanistan.

Part of the problem is that the call for talks is so heavily laden with caveats and restrictions—among them that the Taliban must accept the 2004 constitution and renounce violence and "terrorism"—that it derails any possibility of real negotiations.

However, Taliban leaders argue that the 2004 constitution was imposed from the outside, and they want a role in rewriting it. And they denounced international terrorism five years ago.

As Anatol Lieven—a King's College London professor, senior researcher at the New America Foundation, and probably the best informed English-language writer on Afghanistan—points out, Americans consistently paint themselves into a corner by demonizing their opponents.

That, in turn, leads to "a belief that any enemy of the United States must inevitably be evil. Not only does this tendency make pragmatic compromises with opponents much more difficult (and much more embarrassing should they eventually be reached), but, consciously or unconsciously it allows the US government and media to blind the US public, and often themselves, to the evils of America's own allies."

For instance, the United States will not talk with the Haqqani group, a Taliban ally, even though it is the most effective military force confronting the NATO occupation. The same goes for Iran, even though Tehran played a key role in organizing the 2003 Bonn conference that led to the formation of the current Kabul government.

Iran also has legitimate interests in the current war. Because opium and heroin are not a major problem in the United States, Washington can afford to turn a blind eye to the Afghan government's alliance with drug-dealing warlords. Heroin addiction, however, constitutes a national health crisis in Iran and Russia.

It is not exactly clear what will happen in 2014. While American combat units are supposed to be withdrawn, in accordance with a treaty between NATO and the government of President Harmid Karzai, several thousand U.S. Special Forces, military trainers, CIA personnel, and aircraft will remain on nine bases until 2024. That agreement was the supposed reason for the massive suicide bomb May 16 in Kabul that killed 6 Americans and 16 Afghans. Hezb-i-Islami, an insurgent group based around Kabul and the eastern part of the country, took credit for the attack.

That attack underlines how difficult it will be to forge some kind of agreement.

Hezb-i-Islami pulled off the bombing, but the party's political wing is a major player in the Karzai government, with its members holding down the posts of education minister and advisor to the president. Hezb-i-Islami leader Gulbuddin Hekmatyar is also a rival of Taliban leader Mullah [Mohammed] Omar, and the bombing could just as well have been a maneuver to make sure Hezb-i-Islami has a seat at the table if talks start up. Hekmatyar has offered to negotiate with NATO in the past.

The Taliban itself is divided into several factions, partly because the Americans' systematic assassinations of high- and mid-level Taliban leaders have decentralized the organization. The Taliban is increasingly an alliance of local groups that may have very different politics.

The Haqqanis have a strong presence in Pakistan, which requires that the organization maintain cordial relations with Pakistan's army and intelligence services. They scratch each

© Mike Keefe/Cagle Cartoons.

other's backs. So any understanding to end the war will have to be acceptable to the Haqqanis and Islamabad. No agreement is possible without the participation of both.

Instead of recognizing the reality of the situation, however, the Obama administration continues to ignore the powerful Haqqanis, sideline Iran, and to alienate the average Pakistani though its drone war.

Cutting a Deal

As complex as the situation looks, a solution is possible, but only if the White House changes course. First, the "shoot and talk" nonsense must end immediately, General Dunford's hallucinations notwithstanding. If the United States couldn't smother the insurgency during the surge, how can it do so now with fewer troops? All the shooting will do is get a lot more people killed—most of them Afghan soldiers, police, and civilians caught in the cross fire—and sabotage any potential talks.

According to Lieven, Taliban leaders are far more realistic about the current situation than is the White House. Last July,

Lieven and a group of academics met "leading figures close to the Taliban" during a trip to the Persian Gulf. He says there was "a widespread recognition within the Taliban that while they can maintain a struggle in the south and east of Afghanistan indefinitely," they could never conquer the whole country. Further, "in their own estimate," they have the support of about 30 percent of the population. A recent Asia Foundation poll came to a similar conclusion.

While the Taliban refuses to negotiate with the Karzai government, Lieven says its representatives told the delegation, "there can be no return to the 'pure' government of mullahs," and "most strikingly, they said that the Taliban might be prepared to agree to the US bases remaining until 2024." The latter compromise will not make the Iranians, Chinese, or Russians very happy—not to mention Hezb-i-Islami—but it reflects a deep-seated philosophy in Afghan politics: figure out a way to cut a deal.

The Taliban's rejection of talks with the Kabul government means that going ahead with next year's presidential election is probably a bad idea. An all-Afghan constitutional convention would be a better idea, with elections postponed until after a new constitution is in place.

There are numerous issues that could sink a final agreement because there are many players with multiple agendas. Regardless, those agendas will have to be addressed, even if not quite to everyone's satisfaction. And everyone has to sit at the table, since those who are excluded have the power to torpedo the entire endeavor. This means all the combatants, as well as Iran, India, China, Russia, Turkmenistan, Uzbekistan, and Tajikistan.

And the White House needs to get off its butt. Afghan President Karzai, just returned from an arms buying spree in India, asked New Delhi to increase its presence in Afghanistan. This will hardly be popular with Pakistan and China, and Islamabad can make serious mischief if it wants to.

The ambush in Pakistan brings to mind Karl Marx's famous dictum about history: It happens first as tragedy, then as farce.

The first time this happened was during Britain's first Anglo-Afghan War (1839–42), when Afghans overran an East India Company army retreating from Kabul. Out of 4,500 soldiers and 12,000 civilians, a single assistant surgeon made it back to Jalalabad.

The most recent ambush certainly had an element of farce about it. Four masked gunmen on two motorbikes forced the trucks to stop, sprinkled them with gasoline, and set the vehicles ablaze. One driver received a minor injury.

There is no need for a chaos-engulfed finale to the Afghan war. There is no reason to continue the bloodshed, which all the parties recognize will not alter the final outcome a whit. It is time for the White House to step up and do the right thing and end one of the bloodiest wars in recent history.

> *"The main rationale for military action by the United States and its allies should be restoring deterrence against the use of chemical weapons."*

In Syria, U.S. Credibility Is at Stake

David Ignatius

In the following viewpoint, David Ignatius argues that the United States, in failing to take military action against Syria for the use of chemical weapons, is undermining the nation's credibility and giving other countries the message that the United States can be defied without consequences. Ignatius claims that there is a strong rationale for a limited and focused retaliatory strike. Ignatius is a columnist for the Washington Post *and moderator of* America and the World: Conversations on the Future of American Foreign Policy.

As you read, consider the following questions:

1. According to the author, Syrian president Bashar al-Assad fired chemical weapons in August 2013 where and against whom?

2. The author claims that President Barack Obama's failure to retaliate against Syria has fostered dangerous opportunism for what nation's leader?

3. The author cautions that a military strike in Syria needs to be calibrated with what three regional players in mind?

What does the world look like when people begin to doubt the credibility of U.S. power? Unfortunately, we're finding that out in Syria and other nations where leaders have concluded they can defy a war-weary United States without paying a price.

Using military power to maintain a nation's credibility may sound like an antiquated idea, but it's all too relevant in the real world we inhabit. It has become obvious in recent weeks that President [Barack] Obama, whose restrained and realistic foreign policy I generally admire, needs to demonstrate that there are consequences for crossing a U.S. "red line." Otherwise, the coherence of the global system begins to dissolve.

The Rationale for a Syrian Strike

Look around the world and you can see how unscrupulous leaders are trying to exploit Obama's attempt to disentangle America from the tumult of the Middle East. As we consider these opportunistic actions, it's easier to understand the rationale for a punitive military strike against Syria for its use of chemical weapons.

Syrian president Bashar al-Assad overrode a clear American warning against such use of chemical weapons. According to U.S. intelligence reports, Assad's military last week [August 21, 2013] fired rockets tipped with chemical warheads into rebel-held civilian neighborhoods east of Damascus. Reports from doctors on the scene are heart-rending. Medicine "can't do much" to ease the suffering, wrote one doctor, because the concentration of the nerve gas sarin was so intense.

What did Assad and his generals think would happen in response to this blatant violation of international norms? Apparently, not much, and in a way, you can understand their complacency: Previous Syrian chemical attacks on a smaller scale hadn't triggered any significant U.S. retaliation, despite Obama's warning a year ago that such actions would be "a red line for us."

Here's another thought to ponder: Is it possible that the Syrian chemical weapons attack was planned or coordinated with its key ally, the Quds Force of Iran's Revolutionary Guard Corps? Surely, it was in the loop. "After all, they're running the show," argues a Lebanese analyst who knows the Quds Force well.

The main rationale for military action by the United States and its allies should be restoring deterrence against the use of chemical weapons. The strike should be limited and focused, rather than a roundhouse swing aimed at ending the Syrian civil war. But it should be potent enough to degrade Assad's command-and-control structure so he can't conduct similar actions in the future. Officials hope the strike will make a diplomatic settlement more possible; they don't want a decapitation of the regime that would leave no counterparty for negotiation.

The Dangers of Failing to Act

A second example of the dangerous opportunism that Obama has unintentionally fostered is that of Russian president Vladimir Putin. He's a pugnacious former KGB officer who seems determined to take advantage of our reasonable, reticent president and the fatigued nation he represents. For a while, Putin's chip on the shoulder was merely annoying. But in turning a blind eye to Syria's use of chemical weapons, the Russian leader is undermining one of the precepts of the global political order.

Putin will try to exploit the fallout of U.S. action, just as he harvested the benefits of inaction. But the Russian leader has truly brought this crisis on himself. Back in February in Munich, Vice President [Joe] Biden and Russian foreign minister Sergei Lavrov were talking privately about the shared U.S.-Russian interest in containing Syria's chemical weapons. Russian behavior in the months since has been selfish and obtuse, and I suspect in the long run it will prove costly to them by fostering more disorder in the region.

Obama needs to calibrate his military strike in Syria with two other regional players in mind: Iran and Saudi Arabia. The Iranians surely have read Obama's caution (correctly) as a sign that he wants to avoid another war in the Middle East. Unfortunately, history tells us that an ambitious, revolutionary nation such as Iran makes compromises only under duress. U.S. action against Assad may not deter the Iranians, but it will at least make them think twice about crossing Obama's "red line" against their acquiring nuclear weapons.

Among Egyptian generals, Saudi princes, Israeli politicians and other conservative players in the Middle East, the consensus seems to be that Obama is a weak president—and that they need to rely on themselves for security. Obama won't change that opinion by authorizing a retaliatory strike against Syria. But if he moves sensibly, in coordination with allies, he will at least remind people that U.S. military power is not to be taken lightly.

"The U.S. cannot afford to cede global leadership when the world is confronted with crises like the one currently unfolding in Syria."

The United States Should Launch a Full-Scale Military Intervention in Syria

Ammar Abdulhamid

In the following viewpoint, Ammar Abdulhamid argues that it would be a mistake to launch a limited military intervention in Syria and that the situation there warrants an intervention that would oust President Bashar al-Assad and bring him to justice. Abdulhamid claims that a limited strike would be ineffective and that the failure to act would undermine the US role as global leader. Abdulhamid is a Syrian dissident and the president of the Tharwa Foundation.

As you read, consider the following questions:

1. According to Abdulhamid, a limited military strike in Syria would do what to President Barack Obama's credibility?

2. The author claims that the conflict in Syria has killed how many people?

3. According to the author, the United States must continue to play the role of enforcer of global law and order until what happens?

If the purpose of the looming U.S. intervention in Syria is to restore America's credibility, and more specifically President [Barack] Obama's, which has suffered measurably on the international scene as a result of his foot-dragging over the last two and a half years, then a limited intervention will prove insufficient and will surely backfire.

The Danger of a Limited Intervention

For should the anticipated intervention fail to cripple the offensive capabilities of the [President Bashar al-]Assad regime, a return to the *status quo ante* of strife and bloodshed will take place within days, not weeks. The world will be watching for such a development. Consequently, rather than restore President Obama's credibility, the strikes will further undermine it. This development will also strengthen the position of the extremist camps within both opposition and loyalist forces, as both sides will be able to use such a soft strike as an indication of the lack of seriousness on the part of the international community, particularly the U.S., in regard to managing the Syrian conflict. Escalations will follow, and the impact of the strikes will be forgotten.

The Syria intervention needed, both to restore America's credibility and help ease the suffering of the Syrian people, should go beyond the limited objective stated by White House officials, including President Obama himself. It should not only focus on punishing Assad for using chemical weapons, but should seek to bring him to justice and stand trial for his crimes. It's about time his impunity was punished, and this tragicomedy of errors and mayhem brought to an end.

Indeed, the conflict in Syria may not end with Assad's ouster, and the ensuing transitional period might still be violent. Yet, to give the perpetrator of the bloodiest crackdown the world has witnessed in decades another chance to cling to power or to chart a graceful exit for himself and his partners in crime will make a mockery out of any conception of justice. You don't punish a mass murderer with a slap on the wrist. The punishment must fit the crime.

The U.S. Role in Syria

Whether he likes it or not, President Obama's historic legacy will likely be judged, at least on the international level, specifically by what happens in Syria. By addressing a conflict that has killed at least 100,000 people and dislocated millions more from the narrow angle of chemical weapons, responsible for the deaths of only few hundred so far (though these figures are debatable), President Obama appears unperturbed and unconcerned with the human toll involved. Worse, he seems to be unwittingly legitimating killing perpetrated by more "traditional" means.

President Obama might still have a problem admitting it, even to himself, but in reality, the current mayhem in Syria is in part his fault. For it is his failure to intervene in the crisis when good and bad guys were easily distinguishable and when "a shot across the bow" could have prevented this descent into sectarian mayhem that has paved the way to this point at which waters are murky and choices hard.

But choices still have to be made, and the crisis must be brought to an end before it metastasizes beyond all control. A regional meltdown will not come as a result of a serious American strike against Assad, but as a result of further inaction.

The Need for Global Leadership

Indeed, it is much more than America's credibility that is at stake here; it's the viability of the existing world order, something that remains a project more than a reality at this stage and could therefore be derailed at any given moment. That moment might be looming.

The days ahead will decide once and for all what kind of president Obama really is, and what his foreign affairs historical legacy will be. If Obama's latest act of dithering, allowing for the current showdown on the Hill, is any indication in this regard, then things do not augur well. The move might have certain domestic "calculus" behind it, but on the international level, it only served to make him appear weak and indecisive, in a world where perceptions matter more than reality.

Should the Congress refrain from backing the President, or should it impose even more stringent limitations on the mission's scope, the results will be disastrous, for Syria, for the region, and for global security. For what happens in Syria will not stay in Syria, and spillovers will not be limited to the region. Now more than ever, every local crisis will have global implications. Isolationism has no place in the modern world. For the same reasons America cannot disengage commercially from the world, she cannot disengage militarily from it. Until the UN [United Nations] becomes a more efficient institution when it comes to conflict arbitration, it will be up to the U.S. to continue to play the role of enforcer of global law and order, an admittedly thankless but necessary task. For a variety of reasons, elected officials in the U.S. may choose to avoid making this particular argument clear to the American people, but they are well advised not to lose sight of it in their internal debates. The U.S. cannot afford to cede global leadership when the world is confronted with crises like the one currently unfolding in Syria. We have already seen what inaction can do. Now, it's time to act, and act decisively.

"The best way to deter Assad is not through unilateral military action but by documenting his culpability for atrocities and isolating his regime from the outside world."

The United States Should Not Launch a Military Intervention in Syria

Michael T. Klare

In the following viewpoint, Michael T. Klare argues that the United States needs to abandon its strategic imperatives in the Middle East and avoid a military intervention in Syria. Klare claims that it is America's geopolitical mission to protect oil exports that has led to past Middle East interventions and will entail an inevitably escalating intervention in Syria unless this mission is abandoned. Klare is a professor of peace and world security studies at Hampshire College.

As you read, consider the following questions:

1. According to the author, the United States paid no attention to the Middle East until what point in history?

2. What is Syria's strategic importance in the Middle East, according to Klare?

3. According to the author, the US involvement in Syria will inevitably lead to initiatives in that country by what other interested parties?

Plans for a US-led air and missile attack appear to be on hold, pending the outcome of a diplomatic drive to eliminate Syria's chemical weapons stockpile under international supervision. But the debate over using military force to achieve US objectives continues. Even if President Bashar al-Assad agrees to demands for the swift destruction of his chemical arsenal under international supervision, the White House will insist on its prerogative to employ force in the event of cheating or backsliding by the Syrians. Why this insistence on retaining the option of attacking Syria, despite growing opposition to such action in Congress and the general public?

The History of Geopolitics in the Middle East

Supposedly, the purpose of an attack will be to deter the Assad regime from using chemical weapons against its citizens while "degrading" its future capacity to do so. But, as in the lead-up to the 2003 invasion of Iraq, those who favor military action are also offering up a variety of other reasons: to enhance America's "credibility" as a major world power; to provide reassurance to American allies in the region; to assist the anti-Assad forces within Syria; and more. Similar justifications were used for the US assault on Iraq. And, just as was true in 2003, a deeper, less acknowledged impulse is driving the United States to war: a perceived need to protect America's geopolitical interests in the Middle East.

Throughout history, states and empires have sought to enhance their wealth, power and influence by reshaping the world order to better serve their interests—by acquiring colonies, forging alliances with friendly states, constraining the power of their rivals, and so on. Typically, this drive has united political-military and economic motives: a perceived need to bolster the nation's strategic position in juxtaposition to that of competing states, along with a desire to acquire and protect valuable overseas assets. Much of what we call "history"—the rise and fall of the great powers, imperial conquest and expansion, wars and rebellions—can be attributed to this combination of geopolitical objectives.

For the United States, the irresistible pull of geopolitics has been most evident in Washington's approach to the Middle East—or, to be more precise, the oil-producing areas of the Persian Gulf. Until World War II, Washington paid almost no attention to this region, viewing it as a strategic backwater. Once oil was discovered, however, it became an area of fundamental interest. President Franklin D. Roosevelt visited there in 1945 to meet with the Saudi king, Abdul Aziz, and forge an alliance under which the United States would guarantee the kingdom's safety in return for privileged access to its vast oil reserves. Every American president since Roosevelt has reaffirmed this relationship, and most have also pledged wholesale deliveries of arms and military hardware.

For a time, the United States was content to share responsibility for maintaining stability in the Persian Gulf area with Great Britain, long the region's imperial overlord. However, when the British announced in 1968 that they would be removing their forces from the Gulf by the end of 1971, American leaders determined that the United States would have to assume the British role as ultimate guarantor of the Gulf's oil exports. Initially, these officials hoped to enlist Iran—then ruled by Shah Mohammad Reza Pahlavi—as a junior partner in this endeavor, but when the Shah was overthrown in 1979, they concluded that America would have to go it alone.

America's Mission in the Middle East

Since 1979, US policy toward the Gulf area has largely been driven by an overarching strategic precept: the United States must bear ultimate responsibility for ensuring the safety of oil exports from the Persian Gulf to the US and its allies, and, to that end, take whatever action is considered necessary to prevent other powers from endangering that flow. This was the impetus for US intervention in the First Gulf War (Operation Desert Storm, 1990–91) and the subsequent drive to eliminate [former president of Iraq] Saddam Hussein—at first through economic warfare, later by direct intervention.

America's geopolitical mission in the Middle East has come at a high price: two costly and demoralizing wars, massive human tragedy, and a decline in this country's overseas prestige and influence. In recognition of these losses, the Obama administration has sought to forge a new strategic blueprint for America—one that places greater emphasis on the Asia-Pacific region and less on the Middle East. This shift—what Obama calls the "pivot" to Asia—has been driven in part by growing anxiety over China's rise and partly by a rise in domestic US oil output, allowing a reduction in America's dependence on imports from the Middle East.

But declaring a strategic shift of this magnitude and actually implementing it are two different things: For all his desire to extricate the United States from Middle Eastern turmoil, Obama has been unable to escape the legacy of our past involvement in the region. Iran still poses a significant threat to the safety of the oil flow from the Persian Gulf, and the petro-sheikhdoms of the southern Gulf—not to mention Israel and Jordan—still rely on the United States to protect them from Iranian aggression. To ignore these threats and obligations would be to abdicate America's status as the world's sole superpower and undermine its ability to guarantee the stability of global oil markets (and thus energy prices in the United States).

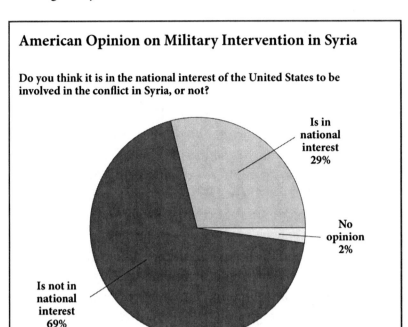

American Opinion on Military Intervention in Syria

Do you think it is in the national interest of the United States to be involved in the conflict in Syria, or not?

Is in national interest 29%

No opinion 2%

Is not in national interest 69%

TAKEN FROM: CNN|ORC International Poll, September 6–8, 2013.

The Strategic Importance of Syria

And this is where Syria enters the equation. Although Syria is not itself a significant oil producer, it lies adjacent to many of the major suppliers and has long served as a host for pipelines connecting the Gulf to the Mediterranean. More importantly, in recent years, it has assumed strategic importance as an ally of Iran and a conduit for Iranian arms shipments to Hezbollah in Lebanon. "Syria has a geopolitical importance out of all proportion to its relatively small population, area, resource base, and economic wealth because of formidable military power ... and its location at the heart of the Middle East," Alasdair Drysdale of the Australian National University wrote in *The Oxford Companion to Politics of the World*. "As a result, it plays a central role in most of the Middle East's key disputes."

This is the dilemma facing Obama today. If the United States cannot extricate himself from the geopolitical imperatives posed by Iran's continuing threat to Israel, Saudi Arabia, and the safety of Persian Gulf oil supplies, it cannot extricate itself from the turmoil in Syria. Because a failure to confront Assad's excesses could be viewed as giving Iran and other outside powers a green light to meddle in the Syrian conflict, and could be seen by the Iranians as an indication that they can continue to stockpile enriched uranium with impunity, US leaders see no choice but to become involved in Syria.

Russian involvement in the Syrian imbroglio adds another dimension to America's dilemma. Russia has long-established ties with the Syrian leadership, beginning with Assad's predecessor, his father Hafiz, and retains a vital naval base at Tartous, on Syria's Mediterranean coast. More important than these strategic interests, however, is Moscow's desire to curb America's global activism. From Russia's perspective, then, Syria is less important as a strategic asset in itself than as an arena in which to gain geopolitical advantage over the West. By the same token, a failure to contest Russia's spoiler in Syria's role could be interpreted as an invitation for Moscow to undertake other obstructionist endeavors.

Add all this together, and it becomes nearly impossible for American leaders to avoid involvement in the Syrian conflict. "What makes Syria so much more complicated than Libya is that the strategic issues are as prominent as the moral ones," said Princeton professor Anne-Marie Slaughter in February 2012, shortly after completing a stint as director of policy planning at the State Department. But while the moral issues may be dominating the public debate over possible attacks on Syria, it is the strategic issues that will, in the end, dictate the government's response.

The Need to Change Strategy

It may well be that President Obama, in his heart of hearts, truly believes that moral—and not geopolitical—considerations should govern US policy in situations like this. Were that, in fact, the case, one could envision a genuine debate over the desirability of becoming directly involved in the Syrian conflict. Under present circumstances, however, Obama is finding it very difficult to escape the geopolitical forces that are pulling us into ever-deeper engagement with Syria.

The more we get involved, moreover, the harder it will be for the United States to limit its engagement to a limited military strike (or the continuing *threat* of such action). Deeper US involvement is bound to alter the strategic equation within Syria and lead other interested parties—Iran, Russia, the Gulf states, Hezbollah and so on—to take fresh initiatives of their own. And, as these will no doubt threaten America's fundamental interests in the region, Washington will feel compelled to consider additional military options—eventually triggering a cycle of escalation whose outcome cannot be foreseen (but is bound to be horrific).

If Obama truly seeks to avoid this sort of quagmire, he must abandon the strategic imperatives that have governed American policy in the region for so many years and fashion a new set of guiding principles, aimed at limiting our overseas commitments and strengthening international norms and institutions. The best way to deter Assad is not through unilateral military action but by documenting his culpability for atrocities and isolating his regime from the outside world.

Periodical and Internet Sources Bibliography

The following articles have been selected to supplement the diverse views presented in this chapter.

Louis René Beres	"Wars Without Victory: The United States Must Rethink the Meaning and Role of Its Military and Security," *U.S. News & World Report*, March 8, 2013.
Patrick Cockburn	"The Absurdity of US Policy in Syria," *CounterPunch*, September 22, 2014.
Patrick Cockburn	"Syria and Iraq: Why US Policy Is Fraught with Danger," *Independent* (UK), September 4, 2014.
Stephanie Condon	"10 Years Later: The Iraq War's Lasting Impact on U.S. Politics," CBS News, March 19, 2013.
Ben Connable	"The Deeply Mixed Results of the Iraq War," *U.S. News & World Report*, March 21, 2013.
Robert Kagan	"The Price of Power: The Benefits of US Defense Spending Far Outweigh the Costs," *Weekly Standard*, January 24, 2011.
Michael Kinsley	"One Simple Rule for U.S. Military Intervention," BloombergView, May 30, 2012.
Stephen Kinzer	"An Extraordinary Turn Against Military Intervention," Al Jazeera America, September 10, 2013.
Michael O'Hanlon	"U.S. Military Intervention, Done Right, Could Boost African Stability," *Los Angeles Times*, February 16, 2014.
South China Morning Post	"US Does More Harm than Good with Military Intervention on Foreign Soil," June 15, 2014.

OPPOSING VIEWPOINTS® SERIES

CHAPTER 3

Are US Economic Policies Worldwide Good for the United States?

Chapter Preface

Foreign aid is a central component of the federal international affairs budget and is often considered a key element of US foreign policy. One of the main justifications for US foreign assistance, especially since the terrorist attacks of September 11, 2001, is national security; although business objectives and humanitarian matters also are rationales. The US government spends approximately $50 billion on the Department of State and United States Agency for International Development (USAID), with foreign assistance totaling almost $40 billion. Assistance can come in the form of cash transfer, equipment or commodities, infrastructure, or technical assistance.

The top recipient of foreign aid in 2013 was Israel, receiving more than $3 billion. Countries in the Middle East topped the list, with Israel, Afghanistan, Pakistan, and Iraq receiving more than $2 billion each, Egypt receiving over $1.5 billion, and Jordan receiving over a half billion dollars. African countries fill out the rest of the top-ten list, with Nigeria, Tanzania, South Africa, and Kenya all slated for approximately half a billion dollars each.

The director of foreign assistance at the State Department developed a framework that organizes foreign aid managed by USAID around five strategic objectives: investing in people; peace and security; economic growth; humanitarian assistance; and governing justly and democratically. In fiscal year 2010, almost $11 billion was spent investing in people in foreign-aid recipient countries, including investments in health and education. A little more than $10 billion was spent on peace and security, which included counterterrorism, security sector reform, and counter-narcotics. More than $5 billion was spent on promoting economic growth, with funds targeting infrastructure, agriculture, and the environment. Almost

$5 billion was spent on humanitarian assistance and approximately $3.5 billion was spent on just and democratic governance.

The billions of dollars spent each year on foreign assistance are controversial, especially since the Great Recession has more Americans wanting the focus to be on domestic spending. A 2013 Pew Research Center poll showed that 48 percent of Americans wanted aid to the world's needy to be decreased, with only 21 percent wanting it to be increased and 28 percent wanting it to remain unchanged. Thirty-four percent wanted funds to the State Department and American embassies cut, whereas only 14 percent wanted those funds increased. Regardless of popular opinion, there are ongoing debates about the effectiveness of money spent in pursuit of foreign policy goals, as the authors in the following chapter illustrate.

"If history is any guide ... the chief weapon in the 'war on poverty' should be not aid but liberal policy reforms."

Foreign Aid Is Ineffective in Alleviating Poverty

Jagdish Bhagwati

In the following viewpoint, Jagdish Bhagwati argues that the impulse to give foreign aid is misguided, albeit with good intentions, and that most foreign aid is wasted. Bhagwati claims that the main problem with foreign aid is that it fails to be effective at its intended goal: eliminating poverty. Bhagwati contends that liberal policy reforms that encourage economic growth are much more effective than foreign aid. Bhagwati is a professor of economics and law at Columbia University.

As you read, consider the following questions:

1. According to Bhagwati, the debates about foreign aid occur largely among whom?

2. What argument was developed in the 1950s to make the case for foreign aid out of self-interest, according to the author?

3. What reason does Bhagwati give explaining why nations that receive foreign aid end up with reduced domestic savings?

If you live in the affluent West, no public policy issue is more likely to produce conflicts in your conscience than foreign aid. The humane impulse, fueled by unceasing televised images of famine and pestilence in the developing world, is to favor giving more aid. But a contrasting narrative has the opposite effect: Emperor Jean-Bédel Bokassa of the Central African Republic used Western aid to buy a gold-plated bed, and Zaire's dictator, Mobutu Sese Seko, spent it on personal jaunts on the Concorde. Such scandals inevitably lead many to conclude that most aid is wasted or, worse still, that it alone is responsible for corruption.

An Indictment of Foreign Aid

These debates have largely been the province of Western intellectuals and economists, with Africans in the developing world being passive objects in the exercise—just as the 1980s debate over the United States' Japan fixation, and the consequent Japan bashing, occurred among Americans while the Japanese themselves stood by silently. Yet now the African silence has been broken by Dambisa Moyo, a young Zambian-born economist with impeccable credentials. Educated at Harvard and Oxford and employed by Goldman Sachs and the World Bank, Moyo has written an impassioned attack on aid that has won praise from leaders as diverse as former UN [United Nations] secretary-general Kofi Annan and Rwandan president Paul Kagame.

Moyo's sense of outrage derives partly from her distress over how rock stars, such as Bono [lead singer of rock group U2], have dominated the public discussion of aid and development in recent years, to the exclusion of Africans with experience and expertise. "Scarcely does one see Africa's (elected) officials or those African policy makers charged with a country's development portfolio offer an opinion on what should be done," she writes, "or what might actually work to save the continent from its regression. . . . One disastrous consequence of this has been that honest, critical and serious dialogue and debate on the merits and demerits of aid have atrophied." She also distances herself from academic proponents of aid, virtually disowning her former Harvard professor Jeffrey Sachs, whose technocratic advocacy of aid and moralistic denunciations of aid skeptics cut no ice with her. Instead, she dedicates her book to a prominent and prescient early critic of aid, the development economist Peter Bauer.

Moyo's analysis begins with the frustrating fact that in economic terms, Africa has actually regressed, rather than progressed, since shedding colonial rule several decades ago. She notes that the special factors customarily cited to account for this tragic situation—geography, history, social cleavages, and civil wars—are not as compelling as they appear. Indeed, there are many places where these constraints have been overcome. Moyo is less convincing, however, when she tries to argue that aid itself has been the crucial factor holding Africa back, and she verges on deliberate provocation when she proposes terminating all aid within five years—a proposal that is both impractical (given existing long-term commitments) and unhelpful (since an abrupt withdrawal of aid would leave chaos in its wake).

Moyo's indictment of aid, however, is serious business, going beyond Africa to draw on cross-sectional studies and anecdotes from across the globe. Before buying her indictment, however, it is necessary to explore why the hopes of donors have so often been dashed.

The Case for Altruism

Foreign aid rests on two principles: that it should be given as a moral duty and that it should yield beneficial results. Duty can be seen as an obligation independent of its consequences, but in practice, few are likely to continue giving if their charity has little positive effect. Beginning in the years after World War II, those who wanted the rich nations to give development aid to poorer ones had to address the challenges of building domestic support for greater aid flows and ensuring that the aid would be put to good use. But their unceasing efforts to produce higher flows of aid have led aid advocates to propose the use of tactics that have ironically undermined aid's efficacy, virtually guaranteeing the kind of failures that understandably trigger Moyo's outrage.

At the outset, aid was principally driven by a common sense of humanity that cut across national boundaries—what might be called cosmopolitan altruism. Aid proponents in the 1940s and 1950s, such as Gunnar Myrdal and Paul Rosenstein-Rodan, were liberals who felt that the principle of progressive taxation—redistribution within nations—ought to be extended across international borders. This led to proposals such as those to set an aid target of one percent of each donor nation's GNP [gross national product], playing off the Christian principle of tithing (giving ten percent of one's income to the church) or the Muslim duty of *zakat* (which mandates donating 2.5 percent of one's earnings to the needy).

How was the one percent figure arrived at? According to Sir Arthur Lewis, the first Nobel laureate in economics for development economics, the British Labour Party leader Hugh Gaitskell had asked him in the early 1950s what figure they should adopt as the United Kingdom's annual aid obligation and Lewis had settled on one percent of GNP as a target because he had a student working on French colonies in Africa, where French expenditures seemed to add up to one percent of GNP. Such a target, of course, implied a proportional, rather than a progressive, obligation, but it had a nice ring to it.

The problem was that the one percent target remained aspirational rather than practical. Outside of Scandinavia, there was never much popular support for giving away so much money to foreigners, however deserving they might be. So aid proponents started looking for other arguments to bolster their case, and they hit on enlightened self-interest. If one could convince Western legislatures and voters that aid would benefit them as well, the reasoning went, the purse strings might be loosened.

The Case for Self-Interest

In 1956, Rosenstein-Rodan told me that then Senator John F. Kennedy, who bought into the altruism argument, had told him that there was no way it could fly in the U.S. Congress. A case stressing national interest and the containment of communism was needed. And so the argument was invented that unless the United States gave aid, the Soviet Union would provide it and, as a result, the Third World might tilt toward Moscow. In fact, the Soviets had already funded the construction of Egypt's Aswan Dam, a project the United States had turned down. The only catch was that if the Cold War became Washington's rationale for giving aid, it was inevitable that much of it would end up in the hands of unsavory regimes that pledged to be anticommunist—regimes with a taste for gold-plated beds, Concordes, fat Swiss bank accounts, and torture. By linking aid payments to the Cold War, proponents of aid shot themselves in the foot. More aid was given, but it rarely reached the people it was intended to help.

When the Cold War began to lose its salience, the search began for other arguments to support aid. The World Bank appointed two successive blue-ribbon panels to deliberate on ways of expanding aid flows, the Pearson commission, in 1968, and the Brandt commission, in 1977. The group led by former West German chancellor Willy Brandt, although emphasizing that there was a moral duty to give, fell back nonetheless on an enlightened self-interest argument based on a Keynesian [referring to the economic theories and programs ascribed to John M. Keynes] assertion that made no sense at all: that raising global demand for goods and services through aid to the poor countries would reduce unemployment in the rich countries—an argument seemingly oblivious to the fact that spending that money in the rich countries would reduce unemployment even more.

Other feeble arguments related to immigration. It was assumed that if aid were given wisely and used effectively, it would reduce illegal immigration by decreasing the wage differentials between the sending and the receiving countries. But the primary constraint on illegal immigration today is the inability of many aspiring immigrants to pay the smugglers who shepherd them across the border. If those seeking to reach El Norte or Europe earned higher salaries, they would have an easier time paying "coyotes," and more of them would attempt illegal entry.

Lewis, who was a member of the Pearson commission, therefore despaired of both the altruistic and the enlightened self-interest arguments. I recall him remarking in 1970, half in jest, that development economists should simply hand over the job of raising aid flows to Madison Avenue. Little did he know that this is exactly what would happen 20 years later with the advent of the "Make Poverty History" campaign, supported by Live Aid concerts and the sort of celebrity overkill that many Africans despise. Of course, this has meant the revival of the altruism argument. Aid targets have therefore returned to the forefront of the debate, even though they are rarely met: in 2008, there was a shortfall of $35 billion per year on aid pledged by the G8 [group of the eight leading industrialized nations] countries at the Gleneagles summit in 2005, and the shortfall for aid to Africa was $20 billion.

The Efficacy of Foreign Aid

One of the chief reasons for the gap is not just miserliness but a lack of conviction that aid does much good. Aid proponents today try to overcome this doubt by linking aid-flow obligations to worldwide targets for the provision of primary education and health care and other laudable objectives enshrined in the 2000 UN Millennium Development Goals (which are uncannily reminiscent of the Brandt commission's proposals). But the question Moyo and other thoughtful critics properly insist on raising is whether aid is an appropriate policy instrument for achieving these targets.

And so one returns to the old question of what Rosenstein-Rodan termed "absorptive capacity": How much aid can be absorbed by potential aid recipients and transformed into useful programs? Arguments that aid can and should be used to promote development seem reasonable but have run into problems—not just because corrupt dictators divert aid for nefarious or selfish purposes but because even in reasonably democratic countries, the provision of aid creates perverse incentives and unintended consequences.

The disconnect between what development economists thought foreign assistance would achieve and what it has actually done is best illustrated by a close look at the earliest model used to formulate development plans and estimate aid requirements. The model was associated with two world-class economists, Roy Harrod of Oxford and Evsey Domar of MIT [Massachusetts Institute of Technology]. In essence, the Harrod-Domar model used two parameters to define development: growth rates were considered a function of how much a country saved and invested (the savings rate) and how much it got out of the investment (the capital-output ratio). Aid proponents would thus set a target growth rate (say, five percent per annum), assume a capital-output ratio (say, 3:1), and derive the "required" savings rate (in this case, 15 percent of

GNP). If the country's domestic savings rates fell below this level, they reasoned, the unmet portion could and should be financed from abroad.

Economists also assumed that aid recipients would use fiscal policy to steadily increase their own domestic savings rates over time, thus eliminating the need for aid entirely in the long run. With such matching efforts by the recipients to raise domestic savings, so the logic went, aid would promote growth and self-reliance.

The problem with this approach, widely used throughout the 1970s, was that although aid was predicated on increased domestic savings, in practice it led to reduced domestic savings. Many aid recipients were smart enough to realize that once wealthy nations had made a commitment to support them, shortfalls in their domestic efforts would be compensated by increased, not diminished, aid flows. Besides, as Moyo notes, the World Bank—which provided much of the multilateral aid flows—faced a moral hazard: unlike the International Monetary Fund, which lends on a temporary basis and has a "good year" when it lends nothing, the World Bank was then judged by how much money it disbursed, not by how well that money was spent—and the recipients knew this.

Poverty and Growth

Similar problems involving the mismatch between intentions and realities are present in today's battles over aid. Now, as before, the real question is not who favors helping the poor or spurring development—since despite the slurs of aid proponents, all serious parties to the debate share these goals—but rather how this can be done.

Many activists today think that development economists in the past neglected poverty in their quest for growth. But what they miss is that the latter was seen as the most effective weapon against the former. Poverty rates in the developing countries did indeed rise during the postwar decades, but this was because growth was sporadic and uncommon. And that was because the policy framework developing countries embraced was excessively dirigiste, with knee-jerk government intervention across the economy and fears of excessive openness to trade and foreign direct investment. After countries such as China and India changed course and adopted liberal (or, if you prefer, "neoliberal") reforms in the last decades of the century, their growth rates soared and half a billion people managed to move above the poverty line—without question, the greatest and quickest progress in fighting poverty in history.

Neither China nor India, Moyo points out, owed their progress to aid inflows at all. True, India had used aid well, but for decades its growth was inhibited by bad policies, and it was only when aid had become negligible and its economic policies improved in the early 1990s that its economy boomed. The same goes for China.

The Need for Policy Reforms

If history is any guide, therefore, the chief weapon in the "war on poverty" should be not aid but liberal policy reforms. Aid may assist poor nations if it is effectively tied to the adoption of sound development policies and carefully channeled to countries that are prepared to use it properly (as President George W. Bush's Millennium Challenge program recently sought to do). Political reform is important, too, as has been recognized by the enlightened African leaders who have put their energies into the New Partnership for Africa's Development (NEPAD), which aims to check the continent's worst political abuses.

But unfortunately, despite all these good intentions, if the conditions for aid's proper use do not prevail, that aid is more likely to harm than help the world's poorest nations. This has been true in the past, it is true now, and it will continue to be true in the future—especially if some activists get their wishes and major new flows of aid reach the developing world simply because it makes Western donors feel good.

Moyo is right to raise her voice, and she should be heard if African nations and other poor countries are to move in the right direction. In part, that depends on whether the international development agenda is set by Hollywood actresses and globe-trotting troubadours or by policy makers and academics with half a century of hard-earned experience and scholarship. In the end, however, it will be the citizens and policy makers of the developing world who will seize the reins and make the choices that shape their destiny and, hopefully, soon achieve the development progress that so many have sought for so long.

> *"Foreign aid may be a convenient political target, but the truth is that our overseas aid is effective, bipartisan, and reflects the very best of America."*

Foreign Aid Is Effective and Should Not Be Cut

Laurie Garrett

In the following viewpoint, Laurie Garrett argues that foreign aid is very American and very patriotic. Garrett claims that recent calls to cut the federal budget by reducing foreign aid are misguided. She contends that Americans believe that much more is spent on foreign aid than actually is the case and that, furthermore, aid plays a negligible role in the budget but a huge role in the lives of people around the world and in the pride felt by Americans. Garrett is a senior fellow for global health at the Council on Foreign Relations and a Pulitzer Prize–winning writer.

As you read, consider the following questions:

1. According to Garrett, total nonmilitary foreign assistance in fiscal year 2011 accounted for approximately what percentage of the federal budget?

2. The author cites a poll finding that Americans believe that what fraction of the federal budget goes to foreign aid?

3. According to the author, what Republican US senator made the argument that foreign aid is good for US security?

I am proud to be an American—no more so than when the ideals of freedom, liberty, and equality on which this nation were founded are espoused by those living in far-off lands. It is our American patriotic duty to wholeheartedly support the betterment of the lives of those struggling overseas under conditions of deprivation, oppression, stifled economic hope, and strangled dreams.

The Truth About Aid

Remove the word "foreign" from foreign aid. We better *ourselves* and bring pride to the nation by feeding the starving, healing the sick, teaching the young, housing the exposed, and providing the instruments of democracy to the world.

So it is troubling to find the first shots out of Washington's budget cannons taking aim at foreign assistance. Critics are calling it wasteful, partisan, and even—at a time of high American unemployment—unpatriotic.

Foreign aid may be a convenient political target, but the truth is that our overseas aid is effective, bipartisan, and reflects the very best of America. Never has its need—or its return on investment—been greater.

The Push to Cut Aid

Total nonmilitary foreign assistance spending accounts for about 1 percent of the FY [fiscal year] 2011 federal budget. Cutting this aid won't make a difference to either debt or deficit reduction. But it will make a huge difference to the hundreds of millions of people who count on US aid for food, medicines, job training, child education, irrigation, small business subsidies, and a litany of other life-enhancing benefits. The gratitude they feel today for American generosity would swiftly yield to contempt and anger for services withdrawn.

Even before the crumbling of the Soviet Union made the United States the sole superpower, President George H.W. Bush warned Americans: "Use power to help people. For we are given power not to advance our own purposes nor to make a great show in the world, nor a name. There is but one just use of power and it is to serve people."

Though she is cut from the same Texas Republican cloth as President Bush, Rep. Kay Granger recently glowed with pride when she told the Congressional Quarterly that foreign aid, "received the third largest percentage of cuts out of the 12 Appropriations subcommittees. The reductions made to my section of the bill are a good start. As long as I am chairwoman of the State and Foreign Operations Subcommittee, I will ensure that our foreign aid is not used as a stimulus bill for foreign countries."

Washington is now in the grips of a major budget war. Republicans, mindful of the hard-line positions they took on government spending in last fall's campaign, are determined to make big cuts, which Democrats oppose. The impasse could force a government shutdown.

Americans' Beliefs About Aid

In this fierce struggle, foreign aid could become a sacrificial pawn. A big reason why is the widely believed myth that foreign aid is a big slice of the federal budget. When asked how much of the federal budget goes to foreign aid, Americans guessed 25 percent, according to a poll conducted last fall by WorldPublicOpinion.org/Knowledge Networks. And when asked what the "appropriate" amount would be, the median figure was 10 percent.

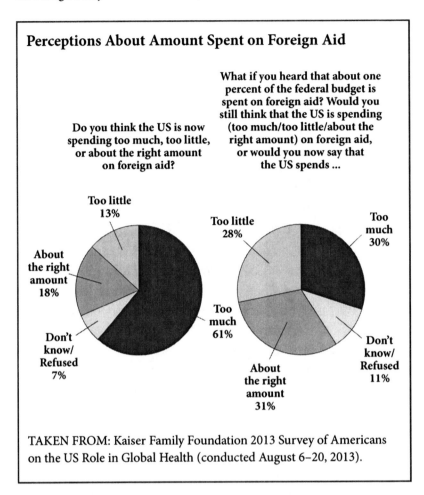

Perceptions About Amount Spent on Foreign Aid

Do you think the US is now spending too much, too little, or about the right amount on foreign aid?

What if you heard that about one percent of the federal budget is spent on foreign aid? Would you still think that the US is spending (too much/too little/about the right amount) on foreign aid, or would you now say that the US spends ...

Too little
13%

About the right amount
18%

Don't know/ Refused
7%

Too much
61%

Too little
28%

Too much
30%

Don't know/ Refused
11%

About the right amount
31%

TAKEN FROM: Kaiser Family Foundation 2013 Survey of Americans on the US Role in Global Health (conducted August 6–20, 2013).

Foreign aid actually makes up just 1 percent of the federal budget.

Congress wants to cut, among other programs: $889 million in food aid and agricultural programs, $1.52 billion from the State Department's global health and child survival program, and $1.2 billion worth of general development assistance. Republican Sen. Rand Paul of Kentucky has even openly called to end all foreign assistance—a call many in the Tea Party support.

The FY2011 total budget is $3.82 trillion, so the $4.4 billion in cuts to foreign assistance and global health represent just 0.12 percent of the budget. Direct global health allocation comes to $1.88 billion, or about 0.049 percent of the total budget. If the goal in targeting development, food programs, and global health is elimination of the federal deficit and debt, these sums play a negligible role.

But the numbers belie how significantly such cuts may impact overseas efforts.

Patriotism as the Rationale for Aid

The GOP would, for example, eliminate about 40 percent of US support for the Global Fund to Fight AIDS, Tuberculosis and Malaria; 10 percent of direct support for malaria acquisition by babies and toddlers; about 8 percent of treatment for people living with AIDS. These numbers translate into direct, meaningful tolls of lives no longer saved, children dying of malaria, and communities unable to obtain safe drinking water.

How can such budgetary slicing be patriotic? As Michael Gerson, former speechwriter for President George W. Bush, recently wrote, "No one can reasonably claim that the budget crisis exists because America spends too much on bed nets and AIDS drugs. . . . The main initiatives on malaria and AIDS were created under Republican leadership. If the goal of House Republicans is to squander the Republican legacy on global health, they are succeeding."

Some key Republican senators understand that supporting foreign aid is essential to US security. South Carolina's Lindsey Graham, for example, tells taxpayers, "We need to be investing in improving people's lives before the terrorists try to take over. Stay ahead of them, not with 100,000 troops all the time, but by partnering with people who will live in peace with us."

National security is a valid rationale for defense of foreign aid. But patriotism is a better one, based in the great pride Americans feel in knowing that billions of people outside our nation thrive because of our generosity. Moreover, they strive to attain the freedom that they see on YouTube, chat about on Twitter, and dream about on Facebook. As Pulitzer Prize–winning American poet Archibald MacLeish famously put it, "There are those, I know, who will say that the liberation of humanity, the freedom of man and mind, is nothing but a dream. They are right. It is the American dream."

> "If we're going to give foreign aid, it should be for political concessions."

Why We Give Foreign Aid

Charles Krauthammer

In the following viewpoint, Charles Krauthammer argues that foreign aid is a tool that should be used by the United States in places such as Egypt to gain political reform, denying that a legitimate purpose of aid is for economics. Krauthammer contends that the only two reasons to give aid are to support allies who share US values and to get others to adopt more favorable policies in line with American objectives. Krauthammer is a Pulitzer Prize–winning syndicated columnist.

As you read, consider the following questions:

1. According to the author, Secretary of State John Kerry gave how much aid to the Egyptian president during a 2013 visit?

2. Krauthammer proposes that foreign aid to Egypt be contingent on what?

3. What four examples does Krauthammer give of political concessions that could be gained from foreign aid?

Sequestration is not the best time to be doling out foreign aid, surely the most unpopular item in the federal budget. Especially when the recipient is President Mohamed Morsi of Egypt.

Morsi is intent on getting the release of Omar Abdel-Rahman (the "blind sheik"), who is serving a life sentence for masterminding the 1993 World Trade Center attack that killed six and wounded more than a thousand. Morsi's Muslim Brotherhood is openly anti-Christian, anti-Semitic, and otherwise prolifically intolerant. Just three years ago, Morsi called on Egyptians to nurse their children and grandchildren on hatred for Jews, whom he has called "the descendants of apes and pigs."

Not exactly Albert Schweitzer. Or even Anwar Sadat. Which is why it left a bad taste when Secretary of State John Kerry, traveling to Cairo, handed Morsi a cool $250 million (a tenth of which would cover about 25 years of White House tours, no longer affordable under sequestration, according to the administration).

Nonetheless, we should not cut off aid to Egypt. It's not that we must blindly support unfriendly regimes. It is perfectly reasonable to cut off aid to governments that are intrinsically hostile and beyond our influence. Subsidizing enemies is merely stupid.

But Egypt is not an enemy, certainly not yet. It may no longer be our strongest Arab ally, but it is still in play. The Brotherhood aims to establish an Islamist dictatorship. Yet it remains a considerable distance from having done so, and this is precisely why we should remain engaged. And engagement means using our economic leverage.

Morsi has significant opposition. Six weeks ago, powerful anti-Brotherhood demonstrations broke out in major cities, and they have continued sporadically ever since. The presidential election that Morsi won was decided quite nar-

Top Ten Recipients of US Foreign Aid in FY2012 (in millions of current US $)

Country	Estimated Allocation
Israel	$3,075
Afghanistan	$2,327
Pakistan	$2,102
Iraq	$1,683
Egypt	$1,557
Jordan	$676
Kenya	$652
Nigeria	$625
Ethiopia	$580
Tanzania	$531

TAKEN FROM: Susan B. Epstein, Marian Leonardo Lawson, and Alex Tiersky, "State, Foreign Operations, and Related Programs: FY2013 Budget and Appropriations," Congressional Research Service, July 23, 2012.

rowly—by three points, despite the Brotherhood's advantage of superior organization and a history of social service.

Moreover, having forever been in opposition, the Islamists escaped any blame for the state of the country on Election Day. Now in power, they begin to bear responsibility for Egypt's miserable conditions—a collapsing economy, rising crime, social instability. Their aura is already dissipating.

There is nothing inevitable about Brotherhood rule. The problem is that the secular democratic parties are fractured, disorganized, and lacking in leadership. And they are repressed by the increasingly authoritarian Morsi.

His partisans have attacked demonstrators in Cairo. His security forces killed more than 40 in Port Said. He's been harassing journalists, suppressing freedom of speech, infiltrating the military, and trying to subjugate the courts. He's already rammed through an Islamist constitution. He is now trying to

tilt, even rig, parliamentary elections to the point that the opposition called for a boycott and an administrative court has
just declared a suspension of the vote.

Any foreign aid we give Egypt should be contingent upon
a reversal of this repression and a granting of space to secular,
democratic, pro-Western elements.

That's where Kerry committed his mistake: Not in trying
to use dollar diplomacy to leverage Egyptian behavior, but by
exercising that leverage almost exclusively for economic, rather
than political, reform.

Kerry's major objective was getting Morsi to apply for a
$4.8 billion loan from the International Monetary Fund. Con-
sidering that some of this $4.8 billion ultimately comes from
us, there's a certain comic circularity to this demand. What
kind of concession is it when a foreign government is coerced
into . . . taking yet more of our money?

We have no particular stake in Egypt's economy. Our stake
is in its politics. Yes, we would like to see a strong economy.
But in a country ruled by the Muslim Brotherhood?

Our interest is in a non-Islamist, non-repressive, nonsec-
tarian Egypt, ruled as democratically as possible. Why should
we want a vibrant economy that maintains the Brotherhood
in power? Our concern is Egypt's policies, foreign and domestic.

If we're going to give foreign aid, it should be for political
concessions—on unfettered speech, on an opposition free of
repression, on alterations to the Islamist constitution, on open
and fair elections.

We give foreign aid for two reasons: (a) to support allies
who share our values and our interests, and (b) to extract
from less-than-friendly regimes concessions that either bring
their policies more in line with ours or strengthen competing
actors more favorably inclined toward American objectives.

That's the point of foreign aid. It's particularly important in countries like Egypt whose fate is in the balance. But it will only work if we remain clear-eyed about why we give all that money in the first place.

> "Sanctions threaten not only to deny these people their health, education and hope for the future, but also to feed new grievances against the United States."

Sanctions Have Crippled Iran's Economy, but They're Not Working

Christopher de Bellaigue

In the following viewpoint, Christopher de Bellaigue argues that the economic sanctions the United States has taken against Iran are causing a humanitarian crisis, turning public opinion among the Iranian people against the United States. De Bellaigue claims that there is very little reason to think that the economic sanctions will achieve the goal of ending the Iranian nuclear program, and he believes the sanctions will simply destroy Iran. De Bellaigue is a journalist who writes on the Middle East and South Asia; he is the author of The Struggle for Iran.

As you read, consider the following questions:

1. The author compares Iran prior to economic sanctions to what other country at what point in time?

2. De Bellaigue contends that prior to imposing sanctions, the European Union used to buy what fraction of Iran's oil?

3. The author suggests that what kind of approach to the Middle East by the United States contributed to the revolutions of 2011?

Iraq before the 1991 Gulf War was a modern despotism with a shiny infrastructure financed by one of the most profitable oil industries in the Middle East. The government provided medical care for the poor; an expanding education system had slashed illiteracy. Life was comfortable for the big, secular-minded middle class—the English-speaking doctors and engineers with their diverse portfolio of investments: property, cars, carpets. The housewives bought filet because it was cheap to buy chuck, fruits were consumed by the crate load, and child obesity was a national problem.

There is more than a passing similarity between the Iraq of 1990 and Iran now—or, rather, the Iran of a year or so ago, before sanctions started to bite. More than a decade of high oil prices had made the country considerably richer even than Iraq in 1990. The middle class splurged on food and consumer goods and the poor were guarded from penury by government handouts. The Islamic Republic earned $166 billion in foreign exchange in 2011 alone, mostly from oil exports of 2.5 million barrels per day. Its leaders were able to laugh off the effects of American, European Union and United Nations sanctions—"scraps of paper," in the words of President Mahmoud Ahmadinejad.

The same leaders now admit that sanctions are having an effect; the supreme leader, Ayatollah Ali Khamenei, has called them "savage." Oil production has dropped sharply for want of buyers and this year, according to the IMF [International Monetary Fund], the economy is expected to shrink for the first time in two decades. In the autumn, the rial lost almost half its value against the dollar on fears that the government is unwilling or unable to prop it up. Inflation is thought to be running at well over the official rate of 25 percent; unemployment is also rising as consumer spending falls and import-dependent businesses go to the wall.

A cloud of pessimism has settled over Iran, with unaffordable rents, empty butchers' shops and everybody scrounging money off the next man. The brash, frenetically consumerist Tehran that I had grown accustomed to in recent years has disappeared. To be sure, Iran is not yet in the condition of post–Gulf War Iraq. The country is still finding buyers for a lot of oil, and the IMF predicts that the economy will return to modest growth in 2013. The various sets of sanctions are far from being a comprehensive blockade.

But nor are those sanctions as "smart" as America and its allies like to insist. Yes, Iran is at liberty to purchase food, medicine and humanitarian items. But cutting Iran off from the international banking system is a sure way of denying people access to foreign commodities, as is deliberately bringing about the collapse of the rial. Already, there are signs of a humanitarian crisis. According to the *New York Times*, one of the last Western media outlets with a resident correspondent in Tehran, Iranians suffering from cancer, haemophilia, thalassemia and kidney problems are finding it increasingly hard to get the foreign-made medicines they need. A charity chief quoted by the paper said that hospital machines are breaking down from a lack of spare parts and that pharmaceutical companies are running out of imported raw materials.

And the sanctions are set to only get harder—more "crippling," in the brutal lexicon now being employed on both sides of the Atlantic. This year alone, hundreds of millions of dollars in fines have been levied against Standard Chartered and the Dutch bank IMG for moving Iranian money through the U.S. financial system. In the spring, the electronic transfer giant SWIFT ended transactions with Iran's banking sector.

The Unintended Consequences of Sanctions Against Iran

Sanctions have had important unintended consequences, including empowering the existing regime, while weakening more moderate, pro-Western Iranians who could be allies of the United States in the future. Paradoxically, economic woes have allowed the government to take greater control over the economy, and to use patronage, favors, and other methods to shield regime allies from the pain of sanctions. On the other hand, those hit hardest by the sanctions seem to be precisely those who otherwise would support a more moderate government in Iran, and who look favorably on the U.S. Reducing the economic and political power that such groups wield is not in the U.S.'s long-term interests as it looks to eventually pursue a normalized relationship with Iran.

Laicie Heeley and Usha Sahay,
"Are Sanctions on Iran Working?,"
Center for Arms Control and Non-Proliferation,
June 3, 2013.

The European Union, which used to buy 20 percent of Iran's oil, has recently imposed an embargo. A new congressional report details how the foreign subsidiaries of several U.S. firms have decided "voluntarily" to stop doing business with Iran. The same report notes that some U.S. lawmakers believe that pressure should increase still "further and faster."

Indeed, the Obama administration presents the sanctions regime a triumph of U.S.-led multilateralism—a coalition of countries adroitly marshalled into action against a rogue state which has refused to subject its nuclear complex to proper scrutiny or constraints. A consensus has emerged that the sanctions against Iran are an exemplary instance of foreign policy. They are supported by the peace lobby because they seem preferable to war, as well as by the hawks, who regard them as an overture to war.

But what is the plan if they don't work? Sure enough, buried towards the end of the congressional report is the mealy-mouthed admission that "sanctions have not, to date, accomplished their core strategic objective of compelling Iran to verifiably limit its nuclear development to purely peaceful purposes."

The assumption is that the more Iranians suffer, the more their leaders will feel the pressure and either change course or be overthrown in a popular uprising. And yet, there is no evidence to suggest that this is probable, and the Iraqi case suggests the opposite. During the U.N. blockade, Saddam [Hussein] was able to blame foreigners for the nation's suffering, and ordinary Iraqis—those who might have been expected to show discontent at his misrule—grew more and more dependent on the rations he distributed. Furthermore, America's insistence that an end to sanctions was conditional on Saddam's departure removed any incentive he might have had to cooperate with U.N. weapons inspectors. In 1997, he stopped doing so, with the results we all know.

This time, the U.S. is at pains to show that the Islamic Republic will gain a lifesaving reprieve if it falls in with U.N. resolutions calling on it to stop enriching uranium. If that happens, Hillary Clinton said in October, sanctions might be "remedied in short order." But Iran's supreme leader dismissed her words as a "lie."

Khamenei and those around him believe the sanctions policy is part of a bigger American project of Iraq-style regime change. There is some logic to this; recent Western tactics against Iran include sabotage, assassination and diplomatic isolation—hardly indicative of a desire for détente. The most recent round of nuclear negotiations foundered, in part, on Iran's growing conviction that the U.S. will make no significant concession on sanctions unless Iran drastically scales down its program of uranium enrichment. That seems unlikely to happen—not simply for reasons of image and prestige, but because, as American hostility sharpens, Iran may judge its nuclear program to be the best defense it has against the fate that befell Saddam.

Washington has been pushing against an Israeli attack and insisting that sanctions must be given "time to work". Unless the U.S. much more effectively shows that sanctions will be lightened substantially in return for confidence-building measures on Iran's part, the danger is that sanctions will have ceased to serve as an instrument of policy, and simply become the policy itself. They increasingly seem little more than an attempt to strike a domestic compromise between doves and hawks—a compromise destined to fail to achieve its stated international aims, while destroying Iran in the bargain.

The current course bucks the hopeful trend seen during most of the first Obama term, when America adopted a sensible, hands-off approach to most of the Middle East, thus contributing to the revolutions of 2011. The irony is that, compared to most Middle Easterners, ordinary Iranians are pro-American. Sanctions threaten not only to deny these people their health, education and hope for the future, but also to feed new grievances against the United States. It happened in Iraq, as we discovered after 2003. Hasn't that lesson been learned?

> *"There can be little doubt that sanctions helped bring the Iranians to the negotiating table, just as they were intended to do."*

Economic Sanctions Against Iran Are Working

John Cassidy

In the following viewpoint, John Cassidy argues that despite the poor reputation of economic sanctions, the recent negotiations with Iran show that they can be effective and are working in this case. Cassidy claims that although there are legitimate concerns about how economic sanctions affect the civilian populace, alongside a credible threat of military action they can be effective. Cassidy is a staff writer at the New Yorker *and a contributor to the* New York Review of Books.

As you read, consider the following questions:

1. What four countries does the author name where past economic sanctions did not work out as planned?

2. What are two examples that Cassidy gives of specific economic sanctions taken against Iran since 2005?

3. The author contends that the success of economic sanctions with Iran is a welcome development after a decade of what default position of the US government?

Economic sanctions have had a bad rap. Ever since 1919, when Woodrow Wilson suggested that boycotting the goods and services of rogue nations could serve as a peaceful substitute for wars, critics have been claiming that sanctions are woolly, ineffectual, and counterproductive. And there have been many times when they didn't work out as planned, such as the sanctions that the League of Nations imposed on [fascist leader Benito] Mussolini's Italy following its invasion of Abyssinia; the U.S. embargoes of Cuba and North Korea, both of which date back more than fifty years; and the U.S. and European sanctions on Zimbabwe, which have been in effect for over a decade.

The Debate About Economic Sanctions

The Castro brothers [Fidel and Raúl], the Kims [Kim Il-sung, Kim Jong-il, and Kim Jong-un], and Robert Mugabe didn't hide their displeasure with the prohibitions that were imposed on their countries; but nor did they change their policies very much. Academic studies appeared to confirm that, in the vast majority of cases, economic sanctions had failed to achieve their goals. In some circles—mainly but not exclusively on the right—it became an item of faith that the targets of the sanctions invariably find a way to get around them, ignore them, or force their unfortunate citizens to bear the burden of them. In the run-up to the 2003 invasion of Saddam Hussein's Iraq, which had been subjected to extensive U.N. [United Nations] sanctions since it invaded Kuwait in 1990, the supposed futility of economic pressures was a key argument made by supporters of the war.

However, in this instance, as in others, it turned out that the efficacy of the sanctions had been underestimated. U.N.

Resolutions 661 and 687, which banned foreigners from trading with Iraq everything except medical supplies and food used for humanitarian purposes, were primarily intended to prevent Hussein's regime from acquiring weapons of mass destruction [WMDs] and long-range ballistic missiles. And this goal, it subsequently turned out, the sanctions had accomplished: contrary to all we'd heard before the invasion, Saddam didn't have any WMDs. Still, even after this tragic episode, many experts continued to cast doubt on the usefulness of sanctions. All too often, a 2006 editorial in the *Economist* concluded, they "make for botched jobs and unbothered dictators."

For the past few years, the debate about sanctions has centered on Iran. In 2005, following the election of the hard-line President Ahmadinejad, Iran expressed its determination to resume its uranium-enrichment program, which it had suspended the previous year. During the ensuing eight years, the United Nations passed a series of resolutions that banned the export of nuclear-related materials to Iran, imposed an arms embargo on the country, and froze the foreign assets of many individuals and entities associated with the regime in Tehran. The U.S. Congress stiffened the sanctions that had been in effect since the 1979 revolution, banning virtually all imports from Iran and even freezing the assets of the Iranian central bank. The European Union and Canada imposed an oil embargo on Iran, and other countries, including Japan and South Korea, both of which are heavily dependent on Iranian oil imports, also imposed sanctions.

The Concerns About Economic Sanctions

Once again, many people said the strategy of squeezing a rogue regime economically wouldn't work. Donald Rumsfeld, who evidently didn't learn very much from Iraq, opined that the chances of Iran agreeing to U.N. requirements for inspection of its nuclear facilities were "close to zero." Ivan Eland, the author of a skeptical book about sanctions, wrote in the *Washington Times*, "If anything, the sanctions are likely to increase support for the regime as Iranians, like other people in similar circumstances of external pressure, rally around their flag."

Even the nonpartisan Center for Arms Control and Non-Proliferation expressed some doubts about the economic blockade, saying its effects, which have included a fall in oil production, a collapse in the value of the Iranian currency, and a big jump in inflation, were mainly hitting ordinary Iranians rather than the country's leaders.

"Paradoxically, economic woes have allowed the government to take greater control over the economy, and to use patronage, favors, and other methods to shield regime allies from the pain of sanctions," the report said. "On the other hand, those hit hardest by the sanctions seem to be precisely those who otherwise would support a more moderate government in Iran, and who look favorably on the U.S."

The report expressed a legitimate concern. But since the election of President Hassan Rouhani earlier this year [2013], the government in Tehran has indicated that it's not just the Iranian populace that wants the sanctions relaxed; members of the regime are equally keen to regain some of their economic freedom. As always, what's really happening inside the Iranian government is somewhat opaque. Still, it seems clear that Ayatollah Ali Khamenei and his cronies empowered Rouhani to do a deal that would see Iran turn over, or destroy, some of its highly enriched uranium in return for being allowed to keep much of its nuclear program intact, at least for now.

So did the economic sanctions work? After this weekend's deal was announced [November 24, 2013, with Iran agreeing to limit its nuclear program for lighter sanctions], that was one of the questions my colleague Jonathan Shainin asked Gary Samore, a Harvard professor who, during the [Barack] Obama administration's first term, worked as the White

House's coordinator for arms control and WMDs. "Yes, the sanctions have worked to pressure Iran to accept temporary limits on its nuclear program," Samore replied. "But whether the remaining sanctions and the threat of additional sanctions will be sufficient to force Iran to accept more extensive and permanent nuclear limits is unclear. . . . In six months, we'll have a better idea which argument is correct."

The Role of Sanctions

Samore's cautionary note is justified. As President Obama and many others have said, this is just the first step toward a comprehensive agreement. But there can be little doubt that sanctions helped bring the Iranians to the negotiating table, just as they were intended to do. Particularly galling to Iran's leaders was the European Union's decision, in April of last year, to ban Iranian banks from the global clearing system that is used to transfer cash around the world. "Iran is a part of the global trading environment and they live economically through the sale of natural resources," Danielle Pletka, an analyst at the American Enterprise Institute, told NPR [National Public Radio]. "So, when you go after their banks, systematically you destroy their ability to get money."

That's an argument for so-called "smart sanctions," which were pioneered by the Swiss and German governments. Aimed at discomfiting the leaders of the target country rather than its economy as a whole, these types of measures include imposing restrictions on travel by government officials and excluding them from sporting and cultural events, as well as freezing their overseas bank accounts. Given the apparent success of such targeted sanctions in the Iranian case, it seems likely that they will be the way of the future.

Does this mean that Wilson was right about sanctions when he said, "Apply this economic, peaceful, silent, deadly remedy, and there will be no need for force"? Sadly not. One lesson we've just relearned is that sanctions are more effective if they are combined with a credible threat of military action. In the internal deliberations that resulted in Tehran's decision to seek out a deal, if only a temporary one, Israel's sabre rattling and President Obama's refusal to rule out a strike on Iran's nuclear reactors must surely have played a role.

But the sanctions themselves were the West's primary lever, and once the European Union, Iran's largest trading partner, agreed to join the United States in ratcheting up the pressure, they proved effective in pretty short order. The doubters were shown to be wrong. After a decade in which resorting to military might to resolve conflicts became almost the default position of the U.S. government (much to the chagrin of many military leaders), that's an encouraging development—and one that shouldn't be forgotten quickly.

| *"Support for Israel has been a very profitable investment for the USA."*

The United States Should Continue to Give Foreign Aid to Israel

David Meir-Levi

In the following viewpoint, David Meir-Levi argues that economic aid given to Israel has been a good investment for the United States, returning much value in the form of military intelligence and strategic security assistance. Meir-Levi contends that the United States has a special relationship with Israel because Israel's enemies are America's enemies, and aid to Israel helps keep America safe. Meir-Levi is director of research at the Israel Peace Initiative in San Francisco and author of History Upside Down: The Roots of Palestinian Fascism and the Myth of Israeli Aggression.

As you read, consider the following questions:

1. Approximately how much economic aid does the United States give to Israel per year, according to the author?

2. According to Meir-Levi, Israel votes with the United States in the United Nations what percentage of the time?

3. Israel provides what safe port as a military base for American forces, according to the author?

Numerous American leaders over the decades have expressed their perception that Israel and the USA have a "special relationship," that Israel's enemies are America's enemies, and that American aid to Israel is money well spent. Most recently, these sentiments were articulated by House Democratic leader Nancy Pelosi, Senator Harry Reid, Vice President Joe Biden, and President Barack Obama. They continue to be in favor of the continued American financial support for Israel, amounting to about $3,000,000,000 per year in recent years.

The Criticism of Aid to Israel

Yet critics of Israel complain that the USA gives too much money to Israel and that the "special relationship" is a liability for the USA. These critics support their assessments with wildly exaggerated claims regarding the size of U.S. aid to Israel, with accusations that Israel is bankrupting the USA, and with the warning that U.S. money encourages Israeli obduracy, stokes the Israel-Arab conflict and generates anti-American sentiment in Muslim countries. In short, they blame Israel for America's difficulties abroad.

While it is undeniable that the enemies of both the USA and Israel exploit American support for Israel to foment anti-American sentiment, it is a grave strategic error to place credence in such anti-Israel propaganda. Yet that is what the critics do, with the apparent intent to undermine the "special relationship."

Since U.S. support is of vital importance to Israel's security, an examination of these critics' claims seems worthwhile.

There are five questions that arise in the context of U.S. aid to Israel and these accusations:

1. Why is there an Israel-USA "special relationship," an alliance which includes generous American aid and political support at the UN [United Nations] and other international venues?

2. What is the real number of U.S. dollars in U.S. aid to Israel?

3. How do we know that the critics offer exaggerated assessments of the dollar amount and spurious claims regarding its political valence and liabilities?

4. What is the value to the USA of its generous financial support to Israel, compared to the value of similar aid to those countries which are Israel's avowed enemies?

5. What is the real impact of the USA's "special relationship" with Israel upon America's position in the Middle East and in the broader Muslim world?

The following [viewpoint] will address the first question. . . .

An Ally in the Middle East

At the most obvious level, Israel is the only democracy in the Middle East. Democracies are an endangered species, so they can be expected to support one another and to have mutually beneficial relationships stronger than those between democracies and totalitarian states.

The U.S.-Israel "special relationship" grows in part from the resonance of a common Bible and a host of Judeo-Christian features. As Western democracies, Israel and the USA have shared strategic interests, shared civic and political values, and the personal, cultural, and political bonds that exist naturally between free peoples. The supreme commander of NATO [North Atlantic Treaty Organization], operations in

Europe and head of the U.S. European Command (EUCOM), General John Craddock, speaking before the U.S. House Armed Services Committee in 2007, called Israel a "model state" and America's closest ally in the Middle East. He noted that Israel consistently and directly supports U.S. interests and U.S. policy in the region.

In fact, Israel is among the few countries in the world, and the only Middle Eastern state, to consistently stand alongside the United States on strategic issues in the UN and in other venues for international cooperation. Israel votes with the USA in the UN about 94% of the time. No other nation holds that record.

But amicable support alone cannot justify tens of billions of taxpayer dollars in U.S. aid to Israel. Happily, the USA has two very strong reasons to conclude that money to Israel is an investment for which the American people get a truly excellent return.

A Powerful Military Ally

First, there is a financial reciprocity in this "special relationship" quite unlike any other that the USA has. Much, and in many years most, of the money that the USA gives Israel has been used by Israel to purchase goods and services, both military and civilian, from the USA, so that American aid money is recycled back into the American economy. Nearly 90% of U.S. aid to Israel is military, and Israel spends about 75% of that buying U.S. goods. This aid has been described as an indirect American subsidy to U.S. arms manufacturers.

But, second, there is more to this issue than merely Israel's using American money to help the U.S. economy. Israel is a very powerful military ally as well. The security cooperation between Israel and the United States is vast, and Israel has consistently been a major security asset to the United States, an asset upon which America can rely, far more so than have been other state recipients of American largesse.

The History of U.S. Aid to Israel

Large-scale U.S. assistance for Israel increased considerably after several consecutive Arab-Israeli wars in the late 1960s and early 1970s created a sense among many Americans that Israel was continually under siege. Consequently, Congress, supported by broad U.S. public opinion, committed to strengthening Israel's military and economy through large increases in foreign aid. From 1966 through 1970, average aid per year increased to about $102 million and military loans increased to about 47% of the total. In 1971, the United States provided Israel with military loans of $545 million, up from $30 million in 1970. Also in 1971, Congress first designated a specific amount of aid for Israel in legislation (an "earmark"). Economic assistance changed from project aid, such as support for agricultural development work, to a Commodity Import Program (CIP) for the purchase of U.S. goods. In effect, the United States stepped in to fill the role that France had relinquished when French President Charles de Gaulle refused to supply Israel with military hardware to protest its preemptive launch of the Six-Day War in June 1967. Israel became the largest recipient of U.S. foreign assistance in 1974, and has only been superseded at various times by Iraq and Afghanistan in the past decade because of short-term U.S. aid aimed at building those countries' indigenous security capabilities. From 1971 to the present, U.S. aid to Israel has averaged over $2.6 billion per year, two-thirds of which has been military assistance.

Jeremy M. Sharp, "U.S. Foreign Aid to Israel,"
Congressional Research Service, April 11, 2014.

In the field of military intelligence, Israel is arguably the world's leading expert in collecting intelligence on terrorist groups and in counterterrorism. It provides intelligence and know-how to the U.S. According to Maj. Gen. George J. Keegan Jr., former head of U.S. Air Force intelligence, America's military defense capability "owes more to the Israeli intelligence input than it does to any single source of intelligence," the worth of which input, he estimated, exceeds "five CIAs [Central Intelligence Agencies]." He further stated that between 1974 and 1990, Israel received $18.3 billion in U.S. military grants. During the same period, Israel provided the U.S. with $50–$80 billion in intelligence, research and development savings, and Soviet weapons systems captured and transferred to the U.S.

Israeli and American intelligence agencies continuously exchange information, analyses, and operational experience in counterterrorism and counter-proliferation. The U.S. Department of Homeland Security and its Israeli counterpart share technical know-how in defending against terrorist attacks, countering unconventional weapons and cyber-threats, and combating the drug trade. On the battlefield, Israeli armaments protect Bradley and Stryker units from rocket-propelled grenades, while Israeli-made drones and reconnaissance devices allow for safe surveillance of hostile territory. U.S. fighter aircraft and helicopters incorporate Israeli concepts and components, as do modern-class U.S. warships. The IDF [Israel Defense Forces] has furnished U.S. forces with its expertise in the detection and neutralization of improvised explosive devices (IEDs), the largest cause of American casualties in Iraq and Afghanistan.

Former Supreme Commander of NATO and U.S. Secretary of State Gen. Alexander Haig described Israel as "the largest U.S. aircraft carrier, which does not require even one U.S. soldier, cannot be sunk, is the most cost-effective and battle-tested, located in a region which is critical to vital U.S. interests. If there would not be an Israel, the U.S. would have to deploy real aircraft carriers, along with tens of thousands of U.S. soldiers, which would cost tens of billions of dollars annually, dragging the U.S. unnecessarily into local, regional and global conflicts."

A Valuable Investment

In short, support for Israel has been a very profitable investment for the USA. Israel is an ideal ally for America in the Middle East. Haifa is one of the safest and most hospitable ports for the 6th Fleet, a dependable base for pre-positioning emergency military stores for deployment in neighboring countries, and a base for close-by sophisticated medical services. In contrast, the problems the United States faces in the Persian Gulf today stem from the fact that it does not have an Israel equivalent there. Absent a strong, loyal, and dependable ally in the region, the United States has had to deploy, redeploy, and redeploy again, at a cost that easily exceeds a trillion dollars. Repeated U.S. administrations came to power predisposed to associate with the Arab world and to disassociate from Israel; but in the end, most came to acknowledge the worth of Israel as a steadfast ally in a volatile region. From Lyndon Johnson on, most have come to see that U.S. support for Israel has been the most cost-effective national security investment for America since World War II and the Marshall Plan [officially known as the European Recovery Program].

In sum, Israel's enemies are America's enemies. Israel fights the same Islamic-fascist terrorism that brought down our World Trade Center, blew up a large chunk of the Pentagon, killed more than 3,000 innocent American civilians, and cost our economy as yet unascertained billions of dollars. Israeli-American strategic cooperation is not a given; it is not automatic; it is not a knee-jerk reaction to shared values; and it is not a panacea; but without it, the world would be a much more dangerous place. Israel helps keep America safe.

At $3 billion a year, that's an incredible bargain.

| "Far from hurting Israel, ending 'aid'
| would be doing America's ally a favor."

The Case for Ending Aid to Israel

Doug Bandow

In the following viewpoint, Doug Bandow argues that aid to Israel is unnecessary and harmful. Bandow claims that Israel is wealthy enough to pay for its own military needs and, in addition, that money from the United States is hurting Israel's arms industry. Bandow claims that foreign aid incentivizes inefficiency and expands the size of money-wasting governments. Bandow is a senior fellow at the Cato Institute who specializes in foreign policy and civil liberties.

As you read, consider the following questions:

1. What is the total amount that the United States has given to Israel in aid over the years, according to Bandow?

2. In 2000 the United States threatened to reduce aid to Israel if it provided weapons to what country, according to the author?

3. According to Bandow, which country announced that it was ending foreign aid to Latin America?

You can't buy love, it is said, but it isn't for want of trying by Washington. The United States appears to believe the only way to demonstrate friendship with other governments is to either defend or subsidize them. Unfortunately, the latter strategy rarely works. It's time for Washington to turn off the aid spigot—especially for wealthier nations like Israel.

Israel does not need foreign aid—it is a wealthy nation with a booming hi-tech sector. Weaknesses elsewhere in the economy are largely self-inflicted through collectivist economic practices. Moreover, Israel is a regional military superpower. If anything, the transfers should run in the other direction. However, the Senate is considering legislation to extend $9 billion in loan guarantees and provide more military support. Rather than reflect warming ties, however, the extra cash indicates an election-year financial raid. Israeli politicians enjoy having more American money to spend while U.S. politicians enjoy spending more American money to win votes.

Yet even some Israelis doubt that American "assistance" is so good for their nation. Last year, Yarden Gazit of the Jerusalem Institute for Market Studies wrote a study that warned "a good many people do not appreciate the real costs of America's assistance to Israel." His analysis suggests that true friendship for Israel would be to set it free.

Washington has provided more than $110 billion in aid over the years, not counting loan guarantees. Last year, figured Gazit, American support accounted for 1.5 percent of Israel's GDP, 4 percent of the government's budget and 24 percent of security outlays. Since 2008, all U.S. aid has been for the military, but money is fungible. Israel receives $3 billion annually, three-quarters of which must be used for the purchase of U.S. weapons. Gazit noted: "While on the face of it, three billion dollars of annual assistance seems fully advantageous, a closer look reveals not a few shortcomings." Money from America has conditions, most notably the requirement that Israel purchase U.S. weapons, which raises Israeli acquisition costs. Gazit estimated that America's "gift" may cost around $600 million. That's a fifth of the nominal "foreign aid." That money, at least, is primarily a subsidy to U.S. arms makers.

Washington also links aid between Israel and Egypt. The latter typically receives two-thirds of whatever Israel collects. The transformation across the Nile could upend the arrangement, especially if Cairo abandons peace with Israel, but so far the relationship continues.

Jordan, too, receives bountiful American subsidies—about $700 million last year. Although the Egyptian and Jordanian grants are a mix of economic and military support, again, money is fungible. And that means American aid frees up resources for Egyptian and Jordanian military use. While the danger of either country attacking Israel remains small, Gazit pointed out that Israel "must be prepared for any eventuality—even one of very low probability—of a defensive war on either the Egyptian or the Jordanian front."

Thus, the more money given by America to Egypt and Jordan, the more Israel must spend on its military. Added Gazit: "With Israel's comparative disadvantage in terms of relative population (over ten Egyptians for every Israeli), maintaining a qualitative advantage in equipment and weaponry is critical." Gazit cited researcher Erez Raphaeli in asserting that every extra dollar to Egypt requires an Israeli expenditure of $1.30 to $1.40 to maintain the military balance. In this way, complained Gazit, "Not only does American assistance not provide Israel with an economic advantage, it requires Israel to expend additional amounts from its own internal security reserves."

There's another problem with U.S. aid. While bilateral defense cooperation has helped boost the Israeli arms industry, the conditions on American aid do the opposite. Since in some cases the Israeli government has to go with U.S. weapons even if the domestic products were better, cheaper or both, efficient Israeli producers lose government contracts and consequent economies of scale. Israeli companies also have to purchase American raw materials, which raise the costs of Israeli weapons in world markets.

Further, notes Gazit: "Due to Israel's reputation as a military power, any acquisition choice of Israel's will instantly increase the demand for that product on the international market. When a foreign country contemplates a purchase from an Israeli arms manufacturer, the question of whether Israel's own army uses that product often plays into the decision." Thus, if the Israeli government buys American instead, Israeli companies may lose contracts abroad.

Washington even uses its leverage to limit Israeli overseas arms sales. For instance, in 2000 Congress threatened to reduce aid if Israel provided weapons to China. "American assistance places pressure on Israel in this area, with the resulting economic loss," says Gazit.

Another impact of foreign aid on Israel is the same as elsewhere—a disincentive to be efficient. The guaranteed payment irrespective of Israel's defense needs "leaves the system with no incentive to become more efficient," warns Gazit. Former prime minister Ehud Olmert argued that Israel could cut its military outlays with no harm to its security but that American money reduces the pressure to do so.

Perhaps even worse is how U.S. "assistance" further inflates Israel's already bloated government. Government-to-government "aid" has expanded the overbearing, money-wasting regulatory state around the globe. Israel is no different.

Explains Gazit:

> Without this aid, it stands to reason that the government would be forced to reduce the public sec-

Aid and Harm to the Private Sector

American assistance is not linked to the Israeli market and is granted to the public sector. Without this aid, it stands to reason that the government would be forced to reduce the public sector in size, through defense budget cuts, restructuring and increased efficiency in other frameworks. This would direct many more resources toward the private sector, which would be motivated to seek creative and growth-oriented solutions, involving personnel, financing, as well as land and other resources currently held by the government.

These challenges and opportunities would pass to private sector hands were it not for American assistance. Instead of helping advance the Israeli market, it acts to obstruct economic growth and promotes its stagnation.

Yarden Gazit, "Economic and Strategic
Ramifications of American Assistance to Israel,"
Jerusalem Institute for Market Studies, January 2011.

tor in size, through defense budget cuts, restructuring and increased efficiency in other frameworks. This would direct many more resources toward the private sector, which would be motivated to seek creative and growth-oriented solutions, involving personnel, financing, as well as land and other resources currently held by the government.

Encouraging a larger and less efficient government naturally reduces Israel's economic strength, which is necessary to maintain an effective defense. More broadly, he argues, "the government of Israel's reliance on the American taxpayer sets a negative example which acts to encourage a culture of dependence."

Gazit worries about the intangible moral damage to Israeli society. He recognizes that budget pressures in America eventually may affect financial aid to Israel. Then unilateral cuts would be seen as weakening the commitment to Israel, yet "if the same move was the outcome of an agreement between the two countries, at Israel's initiative, Israel's situation would not be impaired." Overall, he predicts that "the economic and strategic damage to Israel as an outcome of American aid will only increase."

The financial trials facing America will worsen in coming years. Instead of continuing to borrow to subsidize other countries, Uncle Sam needs to admit that he's broke and stop giving away money he doesn't have. Heavily indebted Spain just announced that it was ending development assistance for Latin America. Washington should do the same, including to Israel. Far from hurting Israel, ending "aid" would be doing America's ally a favor. Israel is likely to achieve its full potential only after it ends its unnatural dependence on Washington.

Periodical and Internet Sources Bibliography

The following articles have been selected to supplement the diverse views presented in this chapter.

Ivan Eland — "Iran Sanctions Won't Work: Effectiveness of Economic Restrictions Always Erodes over Time," *Washington Times*, January 17, 2012.

Dina Esfandiary — "Actually, the Sanctions on Iran Aren't Working," *Atlantic*, October 11, 2012.

Paul Farmer — "Rethinking Foreign Aid: Five Ways to Improve Development Assistance," *Foreign Affairs*, December 12, 2013.

Saeed Ghasseminejad and Nathan Carleton — "Iran Sanctions: They Work, So Keep Them," CNBC, July 30, 2013.

Benjamin E. Goldsmith, Yusaku Horiuchi, and Terence Wood — "Doing Well by Doing Good: Foreign Aid Improves Opinions of the U.S.," *Washington Post*, April 14, 2014.

Hassan Hakimian as told to Toni Johnson — "How Sanctions Affect Iran's Economy," May 23, 2012.

Eli Lake — "Some of Israel's Top Defenders Say It's Time to End U.S. Aid," Daily Beast, July 18, 2014.

Marian Leonardo Lawson — "Does Foreign Aid Work? Efforts to Evaluate U.S. Foreign Assistance," Congressional Research Service, February 13, 2013.

Paul Austin Murphy — "Foreign Aid Is Immoral," *American Thinker*, May 4, 2013.

Christian von Soest — "When Imposing Sanctions, Target the Elite," *New York Times*, November 19, 2013.

OPPOSING
VIEWPOINTS®
SERIES

CHAPTER 4

What Considerations Should Guide the Future of US Foreign Policy?

Chapter Preface

Since the end of the twentieth century, the United States is arguably the sole global superpower. The United States has achieved this position in the world through a mix of so-called hard power and soft power. Hard power involves the use of military and economic means to influence the behavior of other countries: Military invasions, military economic aid, and economic sanctions are all examples of the use of hard power. By contrast, soft power involves the use of diplomacy and culture to influence the actions of other countries: Humanitarian aid and cultural alliances are examples of the use of soft power.

Joseph S. Nye Jr., professor at Harvard University's John F. Kennedy School of Government, has been a proponent of combining hard power with soft power for several decades, resulting in what he calls "smart power." In a 2011 article for *Foreign Policy*, he argues that the United States has relied too much on hard power. He explains that "smart power is the ability to combine the hard power of coercion or payment with the soft power of attraction into a successful strategy. US foreign policy has tended to over-rely on hard power in recent years because it is the most direct and visible source of American strength." Veteran of the Central Intelligence Agency (CIA) Paul R. Pillar argues in the *National Interest* that the overreliance on hard power comes at a cost: "Americans tend to be insensitive to how those not similarly blessed will be attuned to the threatening side of the exercise of power by those more powerful than themselves, and how such exercise may be resented or hated."

Some see the presidency of Barack Obama as making a shift toward soft power. The national security strategy of the Obama administration, published in May 2010, states, "We are strengthening alliances, forging new partnerships, and using every tool of American power to advance our objectives—

including enhanced diplomatic and development capabilities with the ability both to prevent conflict and to work alongside our military."

Critics of soft power see it as no real alternative to hard power. Hoover Institution fellow Bruce Thornton argues in the *Hoover Digest*, "Obama's claims to resolve conflicts through diplomatic negotiations, absent a credible threat of force, are dubious at best." Jim Lacey, professor of strategic studies at the Marine Corps War College, sees the pursuit of smart power as naïve. He argues that it is hard power that matters: "If the United States is going to continue influencing global events it requires hard power—a military—second to none."

The argument about the use of hard power and soft power is one of the many debates about the principles that ought to guide the future of US foreign policy. Many Americans are war-weary, especially in light of the economic realities of the Great Recession, but many policy analysts continue to push for a strong military and the willingness to intervene around the world. As it stands, the direction of future US foreign policy lacks any clear consensus. The following chapter discusses considerations that ought to guide future US foreign policy initiatives.

> *"We will act, and we will do harm despite ourselves. It behooves us, then, to act with humility."*

A Little Humility: If Iraq Has Taught Us Anything, Let It Be This

James Traub

In the following viewpoint, James Traub argues that the aftermath of the Iraq War shows that the attempt at nation building there has probably been a failure, despite wishes to the contrary. Traub claims that the lesson from the failed war in Iraq is that the United States is not always able to help create democracy through war or intervention, though he says it sometimes does, and that this ought to result in some humility in pursuing nation building elsewhere. Traub is a contributing writer for the New York Times Magazine.

As you read, consider the following questions:

1. What is the total Iraqi and American death toll of the Iraq War, according to Traub?

2. Traub gives what four examples of countries where democracy arose in the aftermath of military interventions?

3. What ethnic group in Iraq boycotted the first elections after the war, according to Traub?

President Barack Obama has treated Iraq like a gambling debt inherited from a reckless uncle, steadily whittling down his exposure until he could finally walk away with a sigh of relief. That moment appeared to arrive earlier this month, when the U.S. withdrew its last combat troops from Iraq and the country's prime minister, Nouri al-Maliki, visited the White House, where Obama pronounced Iraq "sovereign, self-reliant, and democratic." Alas, events quickly proved that Iraq wasn't democratic, and possibly not self-reliant either. A better analogy for this tormented country might be the Shakespearean ghost that cannot be willed away.

In recent days, in fact, Iraq has oscillated between farce and tragedy. Maliki had no sooner returned to Baghdad than he issued an arrest warrant for his own vice president, Tareq al-Hashemi, on charges that he used his guards as a death squad. Hashimi promptly took refuge in Kurdistan, and Maliki demanded that the Kurds hand him over or face unspecified "problems." He also threatened to evict his coalition partners if they didn't end a boycott of the government, which was itself a consequence of his refusal to share power with them. And then came a dreadful reminder of Iraq's enduring vulnerability—a wave of coordinated bombings in Baghdad that killed at least 63 people and bore the earmarks of al Qaeda.

Iraq has endured so much violence, and so much political chaos, that this week's calamities do not, by themselves, endanger the state. A senior administration official I spoke to insisted that this "latest spasm of political immaturity" was par for the course, and pointed out that Maliki's political opponents still "see more advantage in sticking with the system than walking away." Vice President Joe Biden, who more or less owns this unenviable portfolio, has been on the phone with Maliki and other senior officials, urging them to settle their differences in private, rather than in the press. But this official conceded that Iraq could descend back into sectarian warfare "if they don't reel this in."

The death toll in Iraq, which has now reached almost 4,500 American soldiers and over 100,000 Iraqis, as well as the cost in money and national prestige, is so staggering that no outcome, no matter how positive, could justify the original decision to go to war. But this week's events also show how unlikely it is that the war will ever come to be seen as a "transformational" event in the Middle East, as New York Times columnist Thomas Friedman recently suggested it still might. Iraq is likely to remain a "sovereign" state, in Obama's phrase, but also a deeply riven, violent, and quite possibly authoritarian one. It will be for other countries in the region to demonstrate that democracy and tolerance of difference is possible in the Arab world.

As the United States leaves this wreckage behind, or tries to, we need to ask, one last time, whether it could have been otherwise. Was the war itself the original sin, or was it the conduct afterwards? What if we had done . . . what? In his 2006 book, Squandered Victory, Larry Diamond, a democracy promotion scholar who worked in Iraq (and whom I cited last week), confronts the original sin argument by asserting that "even with an unpopular occupation, the prospect for democracy was not foreclosed."

The litany of subsequent mistakes Diamond cites is bottomless, and familiar: too few troops, too little civilian authority, criminally negligent planning, marginalization of the Sunnis, the dissolution of the Iraqi army, wholesale "de-Baathification," a compromised constitution, and above all the refusal to swiftly hand power over to an elected government.

© Nick Anderson, 3/22/13, Houston Chronicle, Cartoonist Group.

Each of these mistakes conditioned the environment in such a way as to limit the effect of subsequent positive developments, including the anti-extremist uprising by the "Sons of Iraq" in 2007, and Maliki's bold decision to take on Shiite militias in 2009.

I would like to believe this theory, and for several reasons. First, I don't accept the premise that American power is a blunderbuss that is destined to do harm rather than good. I'm glad the United States and the West acted in Libya, Bosnia, and Kosovo. While of course you can't "impose" democracy, whether through force or even coercive diplomacy, democracies have arisen in the aftermath of interventions—not just in Germany and Japan, but in Panama and Grenada (not exactly commensurate examples, I acknowledge). It is profoundly in the U.S. interest to do what it can to nurture decent governance or even basic justice in places where Islamic extremism has taken hold, or is likely to. And we know now that the truism that "the Arab world isn't ready for democracy" is an excuse offered by, and for, Arab dictators.

I would like to believe it could have been otherwise in Iraq, but I think this modestly hopeful premise underestimates Iraq's afflictions and overestimates America's capacity to cure them. Iraq is not "the Arab world." The Arab Spring has made the most progress in relatively monolithic states like Tunisia and Egypt, and has met with the most violent resistance in places where a minority controls the majority population, as in Syria and Bahrain. Thomas Carothers, a democracy scholar at the Carnegie Endowment [for International Peace], told me that he calls this "the 80–20 problem."

Democratization, he points out, is fundamentally about power sharing; and minorities almost never give up power without a fight. Iraq's Sunni minority had clung to power through unexampled brutality over the half century before the U.S. invasion. Carothers argues that even a larger American troop presence, and a more focused political role, would have been unlikely to have stemmed the rise of the Shiite militias of Muqtada al-Sadr and the Sunni extremists who provoked a civil war in 2006. The increasingly ugly infighting between Maliki, the Shiite leader, and his Sunni opponents, is another symptom of the 80–20 problem.

In the months before the war, liberal interventionists (like me) believed that Iraq could be a just war if the United States accepted the burden of post-war nation building and political stewardship—and then bitterly criticized President George W. Bush for failing to do so. Carothers' point—which he and others made at the time—was that you weren't likely to succeed by fashioning democratic institutions and then training Iraqis to run them, as liberals hoped. If you took power from the minority and handed it to the majority, the minority wouldn't accept it without being cut into the deal—and perhaps not even then. In the end, Sunnis bitter at their fall from power boycotted Iraq's first elections, American administrators helped empower a new Shiite leadership, and today Maliki has declared war on the leading Sunni members of his government.

Perhaps, then, the lesson of Iraq is not, "You must accept the burden of nation building, with all it implies," but rather, "Even conscientious nation building won't solve the zero-sum problem of political power." We should think long and hard about that before, say, we intervene in Syria. But I would suggest a yet broader moral: "We are ignorant." The world is so much more complicated, and so much more refractory, than we wish it to be; and our wishes all too often govern our understanding. It is the combination of limited understanding with immense power that ensures we will visit some measure of tragedy upon the world, and upon ourselves. It can't be otherwise, unless we choose to withdraw from the world, or to watch the worst misfortunes from a safe distance. We will act, and we will do harm despite ourselves. It behooves us, then, to act with humility, and to try as best we can not to confuse what we wish to be with what can be.

"Helping other countries better provide for their own security will be a key and enduring test of U.S. global leadership and a critical part of protecting U.S. security."

The US Military Should Focus More on Foreign Security Assistance

Robert M. Gates

In the following viewpoint, Robert M. Gates argues that the future of providing safety and security for the United States should come from building up the military and security forces of key allies and local partners through security assistance rather than through direct military intervention. Gates contends that to support this goal, there are several institutional challenges that need to be addressed to reform and modernize the US apparatus for building partner capacity. Gates is former US secretary of defense.

As you read, consider the following questions:

1. According to the author, what are the components of "building partner capacity"?

Robert M. Gates, "Helping Others Defend Themselves: The Future of U.S. Security Assistance," reprinted by permission of *FOREIGN AFFAIRS*, Issue 89, May/June, 2010. Copyright © 2010 by the Council on Foreign Relations Inc. www.ForeignAffairs.com.

2. According to Gates, what was the last major legislation passed that structured how Washington dispenses foreign assistance?

3. Providing security assistance that provides predictability and planning for both the United States and partners abroad precludes what, according to Gates?

In the decades to come, the most lethal threats to the United States' safety and security—a city poisoned or reduced to rubble by a terrorist attack—are likely to emanate from states that cannot adequately govern themselves or secure their own territory. Dealing with such fractured or failing states is, in many ways, the main security challenge of our time.

A Complex Challenge

For the Defense Department and the entire U.S. government, it is also a complex institutional challenge. The United States is unlikely to repeat a mission on the scale of those in Afghanistan or Iraq anytime soon—that is, forced regime change followed by nation building under fire. But as the Pentagon's Quadrennial Defense Review recently concluded, the United States is still likely to face scenarios requiring a familiar tool kit of capabilities, albeit on a smaller scale. In these situations, the effectiveness and credibility of the United States will only be as good as the effectiveness, credibility, and sustainability of its local partners.

This strategic reality demands that the U.S. government get better at what is called "building partner capacity": helping other countries defend themselves or, if necessary, fight alongside U.S. forces by providing them with equipment, training, or other forms of security assistance. This is something that the United States has been doing in various ways for nearly three-quarters of a century. It dates back to the period before the United States entered World War II, when [former prime minister of the United Kingdom] Winston Churchill famously said, "Give us the tools, and we will finish the job." Through the Lend-Lease program [formally known as an Act to Further Promote the Defense of the United States], the United States sent some $31 billion worth of supplies (in 1940s dollars) to the United Kingdom over the course of the war. U.S. aid to the Soviet Union during those years exceeded $11 billion, including hundreds of thousands of trucks and thousands of tanks, aircraft, and artillery pieces.

Building up the military and security forces of key allies and local partners was also a major component of U.S. strategy in the Cold War, first in Western Europe, then in Greece, South Korea, and elsewhere. One of the major tenets of President Richard Nixon's national security strategy, the Nixon Doctrine, was to use military and economic assistance to help U.S. partners and allies resist Soviet-sponsored insurgencies without using U.S. troops in the kind of military interventions that had proved so costly and controversial in Korea and Vietnam.

U.S. Instruments of Power

The global security environment has changed radically since then, and today it is more complex, more unpredictable, and, even without a superpower adversary, in many ways more dangerous. The U.S. military, although resilient in spirit and magnificent in performance, is under stress and strain fighting two wars and confronting diffuse challenges around the globe. More broadly, there continues to be a struggle for legitimacy, loyalty, and power across the Islamic world between modernizing, moderate forces and the violent, extremist organizations epitomized by al Qaeda, the Taliban, and other such groups. In these situations, building the governance and security capacity of other countries must be a critical element of U.S. national security strategy.

For the most part, however, the United States' instruments of national power—military and civilian—were set up in a different era for a very different set of threats. The U.S. military was designed to defeat other armies, navies, and air forces, not to advise, train, and equip them. Likewise, the United States' civilian instruments of power were designed primarily to manage relationships between states, rather than to help build states from within.

The recent history of U.S. dealings with Afghanistan and Pakistan exemplifies the challenges the United States faces. In the decade before 9/11 [referring to the September 11, 2001, terrorist attacks on the United States], the United States essentially abandoned Afghanistan to its fate. At the same time, Washington cut off military-to-military exchange and training programs with Pakistan, for well-intentioned but ultimately shortsighted—and strategically damaging—reasons.

In the weeks and months following the 9/11 attacks, the U.S. government faced a number of delays in getting crucial efforts off the ground—from reimbursing the Pakistanis for their support (such as their provision of overflight rights to U.S. military aircraft) to putting in place a formal Afghan military. The security assistance system, which was designed for the more predictable requirements of the Cold War, proved unequal to the task. The U.S. government had to quickly assemble from scratch various urgently needed resources and programs. And even after establishing funding streams and authorities, the military services did not prioritize efforts to train the Afghan and, later, the Iraqi security forces, since such assignments were not considered career enhancing for ambitious young officers. Instead, the military relied heavily on contractors and reservists for these tasks.

More recently, the advisory missions in both the Afghan and the Iraqi campaigns have received the attention they deserve—in leadership, resources, and personnel. Within the military, advising and mentoring indigenous security forces is moving from the periphery of institutional priorities, where it was considered the province of the special forces, to being a key mission for the armed forces as a whole. The U.S. Army has established specialized advisory and assistance brigades—now the main forces in Iraq—and is adjusting its promotion and assignment procedures to account for the importance of this mission; the U.S. Air Force is fielding a fleet of light fighter jets and transport aircraft optimized to train and assist local partners, and it recently opened a school to train U.S. airmen to advise other nations' air forces; and the U.S. Navy is working with African countries to improve their ability to combat smuggling, piracy, and other threats to maritime security.

A Challenge in Building Partner Capacity

One institutional challenge we face at the Pentagon is that the various functions for building partner capacity are scattered across different parts of the military. An exception is the air force, where most of these functions—from foreign military sales to military training exchanges—are grouped under one civilian executive (the equivalent of a three-star general) to better coordinate them with larger goals and national strategy. This more integrated and consolidated approach makes better sense for the Pentagon and for the government as a whole.

The United States has made great strides in building up the operational capacity of its partners by training and equipping troops and mentoring them in the field. But there has not been enough attention paid to building the institutional capacity (such as defense ministries) or the human capital (including leadership skills and attitudes) needed to sustain security over the long term.

The United States now recognizes that the security sectors of at-risk countries are really systems of systems tying together the military, the police, the justice system, and other governance and oversight mechanisms. As such, building a partner's overall governance and security capacity is a shared responsibility across multiple agencies and departments of the

173

US Foreign Policy

U.S. national security apparatus—and one that requires flexible, responsive tools that provide incentives for cooperation. Operations against extremist groups in the Philippines and, more recently, Yemen have shown how well-integrated training and assistance efforts can achieve real success.

But for all the improvements of recent years, the United States' interagency tool kit is still a hodgepodge of jury-rigged arrangements constrained by a dated and complex patchwork of authorities, persistent shortfalls in resources, and unwieldy processes. The National Security Act that created most of the current interagency structure was passed in 1947, the last major legislation structuring how Washington dispenses foreign assistance was signed by President John F. Kennedy, and the law governing U.S. exports of military equipment was passed in 1976. All the while, other countries that do not suffer from such encumbrances have been more quickly funding projects, selling weapons, and building relationships.

A Plan for Moving Forward

In 2005, to address the country's most pressing needs, the Defense Department obtained authorities that enable the military to respond to unforeseen threats and opportunities by providing training and equipment to other countries with urgent security needs. These new tools came with an important innovation: their use requires the concurrence of both the secretary of defense and the secretary of state in what is called a "dual key" decision-making process. In recent years, the secretaries have used these authorities to assist the Lebanese army, the Pakistani special forces, and the navies and maritime security forces of Indonesia, Malaysia, and the Philippines.

Those authorities and programs—and the role of the Defense Department in foreign assistance writ large—have stirred debates across Washington. I never miss an opportunity to call for more funding for diplomacy and development and for a greater emphasis on civilian programs. I also once warned

174

The Importance of Security Assistance

As U.S. forces begin to come home after years at war, the United States has a chance to look ahead to the security challenges and opportunities of the future. At the same time, putting our fiscal house in order is a matter of national security. Even as we undertake responsible reductions in federal spending, it is critical that the United States continue to empower its allies and partners to address common security challenges. More and more countries are seeking to partner with the United States, especially in the security sector, providing the United States with a strategic opportunity to build new partnerships and strengthen existing ones. Security assistance programs—from direct military grants to arms transfers—will be critical tools to seize these opportunities, advance U.S. global leadership and stability. Investments in these areas can pay long-term dividends. Via security assistance, the United States can transform cautious partners into long-term allies and make existing allies more capable. This will be critical in the years ahead.

Andrew J. Shapiro,
"A New Era for US Security Assistance,"
Washington Quarterly, Fall 2012.

publicly of a "creeping militarization" of aspects of U.S. foreign policy if imbalances within the national security system were not addressed. As a career CIA [Central Intelligence Agency] officer who watched the military's role in intelligence grow ever larger, I am keenly aware that the Defense Department, because of its sheer size, is not only the 800-pound gorilla of the U.S. government but one with a sometimes very active pituitary gland.

Nonetheless, it is time to move beyond the ideological debates and bureaucratic squabbles that have in the past characterized the issue of building partner capacity and move forward with a set of solutions that can address what will be a persistent and enduring challenge. Last year [2009], I sent Secretary of State Hillary Clinton one proposal that I see as a starting point for discussion of the way ahead. It would involve pooled funds set up for security capacity building, stabilization, and conflict prevention. Both the State Department and the Defense Department would contribute to these funds, and no project could move forward without the approval of both agencies. A number of other countries—in particular the United Kingdom, the primary model for this proposal—have found that using pooled funds from different ministries is an effective way of dealing with fragile or failing states. What I find compelling about this approach is that it would create incentives for collaboration between different agencies of the government, unlike the existing structure and processes left over from the Cold War, which often conspire to hinder true whole-of-government approaches.

Principles of Security Assistance

Whatever approach we take to reforming and modernizing the United States' apparatus for building partner capacity, it should be informed by several principles. First, it must provide agility and flexibility. Under normal budgeting and programming cycles, a budget is put together one year, considered and passed by Congress in the next, and then executed in the third. This is appropriate and manageable for predictable, ongoing requirements. But as recent history suggests, it is not well suited to dealing with the emerging and unforeseen threats—or opportunities—often found in failed and failing states.

Second, there must be effective oversight mechanisms that allow Congress to carry out its constitutional responsibility to ensure that these funds are spent properly. Tools that foster cooperation across the executive branch could also enhance cooperation across the jurisdictional boundaries of congressional committees—thereby actually strengthening congressional oversight in the national security arena.

Third, security assistance efforts must be conducted steadily and over the long term so as to provide some measure of predictability and planning for the U.S. government and, what is more significant, for its partners abroad. Convincing other countries and leaders to be partners of the United States, often at great political and physical risk, ultimately depends on proving that the United States is capable of being a reliable partner over time. To be blunt, this means that the United States cannot cut off assistance and relationships every time a country does something Washington dislikes or disagrees with.

Fourth, any government decision in this area should reinforce the State Department's leading role in crafting and conducting U.S. foreign policy, including the provision of foreign assistance, of which building security capacity is a key part. Proper coordination procedures will ensure that urgent requirements for military capacity building do not undermine the United States' overarching foreign policy priorities.

Finally, everything must be suffused with strong doses of modesty and realism. When all is said and done, there are limits to what the United States can do to influence the direction of radically different countries and cultures. And even the most enlightened and modernized interagency apparatus is still a bureaucracy, prone to the same parochial and self-serving tendencies as the system it has replaced.

Helping other countries better provide for their own security will be a key and enduring test of U.S. global leadership and a critical part of protecting U.S. security, as well. Improving the way the U.S. government executes this vital mission must be an important national priority.

"*Far too much US attention still focuses on 'terrorism' at a time the US faces a much broader range of threats.*"

The United States Needs to Adopt Different Methods for Intervention

Anthony H. Cordesman

In the following viewpoint, Anthony H. Cordesman argues that the United States never really fought a war on terrorism and that the wars in Iraq and Afghanistan were military interventions of armed nation building. Cordesman claims that instability is a problem in virtually every state in the Middle East and North Africa, and he proposes that the United States develop a new strategy that works closely with host countries to address this without resorting to the commitment of US forces. Cordesman holds the Arleigh A. Burke Chair in Strategy at the Center for Strategic and International Studies.

As you read, consider the following questions:

1. According to Cordesman, what amount is spent by the federal government annually on activities it deems as related to terrorism?

Anthony H. Cordesman, Executive Summary, "Changing US Security Strategy: The Search for Stability and the 'Non-War' Against 'Non-Terrorism,'" Center for Strategic and International Studies, 2013, V–IX. Copyright © 2013 by Center for Strategic and International Studies. All rights reserved. Reproduced by permission.

2. The author claims that most of the violence that the State Department labels as terrorism is actually what?

3. Cordesman claims that the United States will have far more chance of success in achieving regional stability if it does what?

More than a decade into the "war on terrorism," much of the political debate in the US is still fixated on the legacy of 9/11 [referring to the September 11, 2001, terrorist attacks on the United States]. US politics has a partisan fixation on [the 2012 attack in] Benghazi, the Boston Marathon bombing, intelligence intercepts, and Guantánamo [Bay detention camp]. Far too much US attention still focuses on "terrorism" at a time the US faces a much broader range of threats from the instability in the Middle East and North Africa (MENA) and Islamic world.

The War on Terrorism

Moreover, much of the US debate ignores the fact that the US has not actually fought a "war on terrorism" over the last decade, and the US failures in using military force and civil aid in Afghanistan and Iraq. The US has not fought wars as such, but rather became involved in exercises in armed nation building where stability operations escalated into nation building as a result of US occupation and where the failures in stability operations and nation building led to insurgencies that forced the US into major counterinsurgency campaigns that had little to do with counterterrorism.

An analysis of the trends in the Iraq and Afghan conflicts shows that the US has not been fighting a war on terrorism since [Osama] bin Laden and al-Qaida central were driven into Pakistan in December 2001. The US invaded Afghanistan and Iraq and then made stability operations and armed nation building its key goals. It was US mishandling of these exercises in armed nation building that led to major counterinsurgency campaigns although—at least in the case of Afghanistan—the US continued to label its military operations as a struggle against "terrorism."

By 2013, the US had committed well over $1.4 trillion to these exercises in Afghanistan and Iraq. At the same time, the US made massive increases in its domestic spending on homeland defense that it rationalized as part of the fight against terrorism but often had little or nothing to do with any aspect of counterterrorism. At the same time, the US failed to develop consistent or useful unclassified statistics on the patterns in terrorism and its counterterrorism activities. The US government has never provided a meaningful break out of federal activities and spending at home or abroad which actually focus on terrorism, or any unclassified measures of effectiveness.

Metrics on Terrorism

The OMB [Office of Management and Budget] has lumped a wide range of activities that have no relation to terrorism in its reporting on the president's budget request—activities whose total cost now approach $60 billion a year. The Department of Defense has never provided a meaningful estimate of the total cost of the wars in Afghanistan and Iraq, or a break out of the small portion of total overseas contingency operations (OCO) spending actually spent on counterterrorism versus counterinsurgency. The State Department and US intelligence community provide no meaningful unclassified data on the cost of their counterterrorism effort and it is unclear that they have developed any metrics at any level that show the cost-benefits of their activities.

The annual US State Department country reports on terrorism come as close to an unclassified report on the status of terrorism as the US government provides. While many portions are useful, the designation of terrorist movements is often political and shows the US designation of terrorist movements conflates terrorism and insurgency.

The closest the US has come to developing any metrics on terrorism has been to develop an unclassified database in the National Counterterrorism Center (NCTC) that never distinguished terrorism from insurgency.

This database formed the core of the statistical annex to State Department reporting, but has since been withdrawn without explanation. As this analysis shows in detail, it now has been replaced by a contractor effort that makes all of the previous mistakes made by the NCTC. The end result is a set of official reporting and statistics in the annex to the State Department report where "terrorism" remains poorly defined, badly structured, ignored in parts of the world, and conflates terrorism with counterinsurgency, instability, and civil war.

A review of the Afghan, Iraq conflicts, and other recent conflicts in the MENA region shows just how serious these problems are in distorting the true nature of the wars the US is fighting and the threats it faces. The same is true of the unclassified reporting the US government provides on terrorism. A detailed review of the most recent State Department report on terrorism provides important insights into key terrorist movements, but the narratives generally ignore their ties to insurgent movements, their statistical data include some major insurgent movements and exclude others, and many of the data seem to include violence that is not truly terroristic in character.

Instability, Insurgency, and Civil Violence

Terrorism does remain a very real threat. There is enough official reporting on attempted acts of terrorism in the US to make this clear, as does the tragedy of the Boston Marathon [in 2013, when three people died and hundreds of others were injured when homemade bombs exploded]. At the same time, the administration has implied a level of success in dealing with al-Qaida that does not exist.

The narratives in the State Department's latest annual report on terrorism have many limits—including the failure to analyze the causes of extremist activity and distinguish terrorism from insurgency. They are all too correct, however, in showing that that the US has not defeated al-Qaida. They show that US has not defeated the various extremist groups that blur the line between terrorism and insurgency in Iraq. They also show that the US will not defeat "terrorism" in Afghanistan and Pakistan as it exits the counterinsurgency struggle in Afghanistan, and the US faces a growing number of other violent extremist movements.

Most of the violence that the State Department labels as terrorism is actually some form of insurgency, rather than purely terrorism. It is not the product of marginal or extremist ideology, or some form of international terrorist activity, but is driven by deep internal causes of instability in the countries involved.

The violent non-state actors seeking power in given countries are far more characteristic of insurgents than terrorists. In many cases, the state is guilty of its own forms of terrorism, major human rights abuses, or been a case source of civil discontent and violence. Most of the violent movements involved—including most of the "terrorist" movements listed in the State Department report—are largely domestic and only use international attacks peripherally in an effort to win national battle. Many violent insurgent groups—as has been the case in Libya and is now the case in Syria—do not threaten US interests and may advance them.

Instability in MENA Countries

The key challenge the US now faces in the Middle East and North Africa (MENA) and the Islamic world is not to fight "wars" to defeat terrorism. It is rather to help create stability in a broad range of MENA countries where violence is only one major challenge. As studies like the Arab development re-

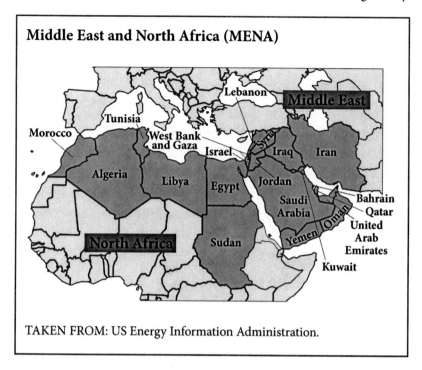

Middle East and North Africa (MENA)

TAKEN FROM: US Energy Information Administration.

port show, many countries would have faced massive—decade-long—demographic, economic, ethnic/sectarian/tribal, governance challenges even if the uprising that began in Tunisia in December 2010 had never occurred.

Since that uprising, instability has become a problem in virtually every MENA state. It has also become a "clash within a civilization" rather than a "clash between civilizations." It has triggered struggles between secular and fundamentalist Muslims and a growing struggle between Sunnis and Shiites/Alawites that extends from Pakistan through the Islamic world. Syria is the scene of a civil war that has linked the tensions and risk of conflict in the [Persian] Gulf to tensions and conflict in the Levant. Bahrain, Iraq, Libya, and Yemen present the constant risk that the number of civil wars will broaden.

Only a few states have reacted to the other threats to their stability and development, and many states that do not have civil conflicts—such as Egypt and Jordan—have come under pressures that have made their demographic, economic, ethnic/sectarian/tribal, and governance challenges far worse.

The New US Strategy

It is a further irony of the US focus on "terrorism," that the new strategic guidance the White House issued on January 3, 2012, recognized these realities. So did the operational portions of President [Barack] Obama's speech to the National Defense University on May 23, 2013—although they were buried in discussion of political issues growing out of past counterterrorism activities.

US strategy does recognize the challenges posed by an Arab Spring where instability has become the Arab decade—if not the Arab quarter century. What is far less clear, however, is that this US strategy has gone from the conceptual level to a realistic effort to implement it. American politics reject "nation building" because of the mistakes, costs, and failures in Afghanistan and Iraq. Massive military invasions and occupations have led to reluctance to use force in far more limited and effective ways. Opposition to foreign aid seems to be one of the few bipartisan aspects of US political consensus.

At the same time, it is unclear that either the administration or the minority of those who advocate intervention in cases like Syria in Congress understand the scale of regional instability or the extent to which it creates deep structural internal problems in many MENA nations the US cannot "fix" from outside. The causes are matters of religion and culture and involve basic problems in the legitimacy and competence of governments. They are the product of deep structural problems in the economy and gross inequalities in income distribution. They involve demographic problems and employment issues, and most involve deep ethnic and tribal divisions that mean the current climate of instability will generally last at least a decade.

The end result is that both counterterrorism and counterinsurgency have become subsets of broader problems in national and regional stability that the US can sometimes influence and sometimes help contain, but that given nations must deal with internally and largely on their own. The US can provide some forms of expertise and security assistance, it can provide limited aid in governance and economic reform, but, there will be no quick solutions, no end to the extent to which violence within the region spills outside it or threatens key regional roles like energy exports.

The US faces other limits. It has other strategic priorities, and is likely to face serious problems in restructuring its domestic budget for years to come. As Afghanistan and Iraq have made all too clear, the US cannot occupy and stabilize troubled states by force. Weak and incompetent US aid efforts have proved to have few benefits and often to do little more than waste money. In both Afghanistan and Iraq, the US has ended in funding dubious attempts at buying short-term stability or funding long-term project aid that waste money on efforts the host country does not need and/or cannot effectively absorb and sustain on its own.

An Effective US Response

Put simply, it is time the US recognized that the "war on terrorism" never really happened, and that many of its approaches to armed nation building have been counterproductive and cannot be rescued by even successful counterinsurgency. The US needs to work with its regional and traditional allies to create new methods and partnerships to deal with complex and enduring challenges to regional stability. These are challenges that will require years of patience and will have limited effect unless the host country moves toward stability on its own.

Though the US still needs carefully focused counterterrorism efforts and to support friendly states in counterinsurgency, it also needs to actually implement its new strategy and put its primary focus on the real nature of instability and civil violence in the MENA region. The US needs to focus on broad-based civil-military efforts tailored to given countries and on strategic patience in doing so. It needs to fund enough civil and military aid to have real influence. It needs stronger public diplomacy and information campaigns. It needs to transform its calls for local partnerships into stronger realities.

The US will have far more chance of success if it works closely with outside partners and helps host countries do it their way rather than try to impose its own values and systems. Its main tools, however, must be US strong country teams that combine civil-military-internal security efforts to work with host countries on a nation-by-nation basis. It will be country teams that consistently help given countries achieve stability over a period of years.

Moreover, the US needs to build a congressional and popular consensus around actually implementing its need strategy for the MENA region and for dealing with the broader causes of instability in the Islamic world. It needs effective, interagency civil-military plans, budget, and measures of effectiveness. It needs to provide suitable transparency to show it has corrected the mistake it made in Afghanistan and Iraq, explain and justify its actions, and show the level of progress it is making.

In the process, the US needs to adopt different criteria and methods for armed intervention, be far more careful about committing US forces, tie all uses of force to civil efforts from the start, and substitute strategic triage and strategic patience for committing large elements of US forces to contingencies where they have little or no probability of achieving successful end states or benefits worth their costs in dollars or blood.

> "American foreign policy is impoverished
> by an 'uncompromising Western
> secularism' which makes the danger of
> religious extremism more likely."

Faith, Doubt, and U.S. Foreign Policy

Joseph Loconte

In the following viewpoint, Joseph Loconte argues that US foreign policy is overly secular, ignoring the importance of religion in international affairs. Loconte claims that studies show that despotism has created religious extremism in countries and that this is a threat to the religious freedom of religious minorities. Loconte contends that to ignore this connection and the religious-ideological component of terrorism is dangerous and simply leads to more religious extremism. Loconte is an associate professor of history at The King's College in New York City.

As you read, consider the following questions:

1. According to Loconte, a recent study observes that religious belief is very important to the fate of what six nations?

Joseph Loconte, "Faith, Doubt, and U.S. Foreign Policy," *American*, June 22, 2010. Copyright © 2010 by American Enterprise Institute. All rights reserved. Reproduced by permission.

2. The author cites a recent Pew Research Center study finding which two governments to be the most restrictive on religion?

3. Loconte identifies what paradox in the behavior of former president George W. Bush in the so-called war on terror?

One of the premises of America's foreign policy establishment, entrenched in the State Department for at least a generation, is that faith is the enemy of rational diplomacy. Under this assumption, religious belief must be tightly controlled or rendered irrelevant: It can play no constructive part in foreign policy objectives. The attacks of 9/11, of course, seemed to validate this view. Religious orthodoxy, of any variety, came to be seen as the source of xenophobia, extremism, and violence. So did the faith-based presidency of George W. Bush. In the overheated imaginations of his critics, Bush was a Christian "fanatic" whose crusading foreign policy threatened global peace and security.

A year and a half into his own presidency, Barack Obama has done little to challenge this secular narrative of American diplomacy. His gestures toward religion—the recent decision to fill a diplomatic post promoting religious freedom, for example—exhibit only the Obama penchant for style over substance. The rise of Islamist radicalism should have launched a transformation in strategic thinking about the role of faith in driving political and cultural change. It did not. The problem, as recent studies suggest, is that American foreign policy is impoverished by an "uncompromising Western secularism" which makes the danger of religious extremism more likely.

That's the explicit conclusion of a two-year study by the Chicago Council on Global Affairs, released earlier this year [2010]. The council's 32-member task force, composed of government officials and scholars representing diverse faith traditions, agreed that religious ideals and institutions can no longer be marginalized from U.S. diplomatic efforts. Their report observes that religious belief is "pivotal to the fate" of nations such as Afghanistan, India, Iran, Iraq, Pakistan, and Yemen—all of which are vital to America's national security interests. Nevertheless, assumptions persist that political reforms must be based on purely secular appeals. "Despite a world abuzz with religious fervor," the authors complain, "the U.S. government has been slow to respond effectively to situations where religion plays a global role."

Team Obama boasts incessantly of a more sophisticated diplomatic strategy than its predecessor. The president's speech in Cairo last June, in which he appealed to Muslims around the world for mutual respect, got rave reviews from left-leaning academics and journalists. *New York Times* columnist Roger Cohen reported, somewhat rhapsodically, that the president's address instantly and dramatically softened the anti-American mood among Muslims worldwide. "What Obama has already done for the United States in the Muslim world is unbelievable," a professor in Tehran told Cohen. "It is not easy for anyone here to attack him." The supposed truce lasted less than 24 hours.

What the White House regards as a "nuanced" approach to religion looks more like a bow to political correctness. The president has called for a "partnership between America and Islam," as if the U.S. government signs treaties with religious entities. He has insisted that "Islam is not part of the problem" of violent extremism, as if suicide bombers recited the Boy Scout oath before blowing themselves up. These dangerous and airy abstractions are no substitute for hard thinking about the spiritual roots of terrorist violence. Likewise, the appointment of a special envoy to the Organisation of the Islamic Conference (OIC), a group that flagrantly supports terrorist activity, is a naive gambit. Ali Alyami, executive director of the Center for Democracy and Human Rights in Saudi

Arabia, warns that this brand of outreach "strengthens and legitimizes" religious extremism.

Meanwhile, the White House has picked a New York megapastor, Reverend Suzan Johnson Cook, as the next ambassador-at-large for international religious freedom. The position, created by Congress in 1998, is an effort to put near the center of U.S. diplomacy a basic tenet of liberal democracy: Religious liberty lays the foundation for stable, moderate, and reform-minded governments. An effective ambassador should bring to the job meaningful diplomatic experience and a reputation for defending religious freedom. Reverend Cook, a motivational speaker who likes to be called "Dr. Sujay," has neither. This all but guarantees she will be marginalized by State Department bureaucrats not inclined to rock the boat over trifles such as apostasy laws, religious persecution, or the negation of basic human rights for religious minorities.

Foreign policy "realists"—many of whom despised Bush's democracy agenda and are now advising President Obama—seem unwilling to face at least one prickly reality: despotism, especially in Muslim-majority countries, has nourished Islamist extremism. Without exception, every regime that foments religious radicalism also denies religious freedom to individuals and groups it considers a threat to its monopoly on power.

This fact is confirmed by the results of an important study from the Pew Research Center, released in December 2009. The report, "Global Restrictions on Religion," draws on findings from numerous human rights groups and government agencies to offer the first quantitative study of how political regimes and private actors repress religious freedom. Covering 198 countries over a two-year period, the study found that 64 states severely restrict religious expression, either as a result of government policies or cultural hostilities. "Looking at how these restrictions play out across the world," says senior researcher Brian Grim, "the region of the world with the highest level of restrictions is the Middle East and North Africa."

Pew researchers declined to mention the embarrassing truth that many of the worst offenders are Muslim-majority states, all of which subsidize terrorist organizations. Saudi Arabia and Iran, both of which brutally enforce Islamic law, are cited as the two most restrictive governments in the Pew study. It bears remembering that 15 of the 19 hijackers on 9/11 were from Saudi Arabia, and that, despite official denials, it remains the chief exporter of the violent Wahhabi ideology. Not to be outdone, the Iranian government is justly called "the central banker of terrorism," overtly supporting groups such as Hizballah and Hamas, as well as stoking terrorist violence in Afghanistan, Iraq, Israel, Lebanon, and elsewhere. The regimes in Tehran and Riyadh are poster children for the linkage between political tyranny, Islamist extremism, and terrorist rage.

A final study supporting this connection, "Homegrown Terrorists in the U.S. and U.K.," examined how individuals become radicalized from within Western nations. Released last year by the Foundation for Defense of Democracies, it offers an empirical look at 117 homegrown "jihadist" terrorists. Lead researcher Daveed Gartenstein-Ross describes several common manifestations of radicalization, all of which are closely tied to religious conviction. They include the adoption of legalistic forms of Islam, a low tolerance for theological deviance, and a heavy reliance on select religious authorities. The study finds that one in five homegrown terrorists had a "spiritual mentor"—a Muslim teacher who provided guidance—and nearly 40 percent explicitly claimed a religious rationale for their actions. The report concludes that theological ideas are "a relatively strong factor" in the radicalization process.

None of this should be news to anyone with a shred of rational thought about religious belief and its relationship to Islamist extremism. Yet the Obama administration's response to recent terrorist incidents—the massacre at Fort Hood, Texas, the Christmas Day airline bomb plot, the failed car bomb at-

The Positive Role of Religion

Religion did not suddenly burst onto the scene with the end of the Cold War; it has been a powerful force in society for millennia. Today, however, religion is playing an increasingly influential role, for good and sometimes for ill, in the public sphere.

Much is heard about the radical and dangerous, destructive face of religion. Less well known, but no less important for the future, is the recent emergence of local as well as transnational religious actors and faith-based organizations that are embracing the role of peace builder and of advocate for democracy and human rights. For decades, religious leaders have played a recognized role in brokering the peace in conflict zones such as Mozambique and Mindanao, Guatemala and Algeria. They built and helped sustain processes to advance reconciliation in divided societies such as South Africa and Northern Ireland. Religious leaders such as Pope John Paul II have played critical roles in collapsing authoritarian regimes and facilitating peaceful political change toward democracy.

Chicago Council on Global Affairs,
"Engaging Religious Communities Abroad:
A New Imperative for U.S. Foreign Policy," 2010.

tempt in New York's Times Square—was anything but enlightened. In each case, the White House initially treated the perpetrators as lone, disturbed vigilantes with no connection to Islamist ideology, al Qaeda, or its vast terrorist network. In each case, the secular political reflex proved dead wrong.

Thus, for all its protests to the contrary, team Obama is duplicating a major blunder that occurred during much of the

Bush administration: denying, in practice, the religious-ideological component to terrorism. It was not until Bush's second term—four years after the 9/11 attacks—that Secretary of State Condoleezza Rice initiated a "strategic dialogue" with high-level Saudi officials. None of the working groups involved in the talks confronted the problem of religious extremism. In the months following the overthrow of Saddam Hussein, the White House failed to build relationships with leading moderate clerics in Iraq; extremists filled the vacuum. Entities such as the State Department, the U.S. Agency for International Development, and the National Endowment for Democracy—all supposedly involved in a war of ideas—too often failed to show up for the fight. It was as though religious belief played no meaningful role in Bush's "war on terror."

Hence the paradox: One of America's most religious presidents failed to take religion seriously while confronting a national security threat manifestly rooted in faith commitment. Obama and company have drawn exactly the wrong lesson from the Bush administration. Far from being too religious, the Bush White House was not religious enough.

The Obama administration, steeped in Enlightenment myths about democracy and international politics, is deepening the problem. The White House has released a new National Security Strategy, for example, that deletes any references to Islam or Islamist extremism to describe the terrorist threat. Attorney General Eric Holder, with Orwellian audacity, pretended in testimony before the House Judiciary Committee that Islam had virtually nothing to do with the recent terrorist plots in the United States: "There are a variety of reasons why people do these things." President Obama recently signed into law the Daniel Pearl Freedom of the Press Act, honoring the *Wall Street Journal* reporter who was abducted and beheaded in 2002 in Pakistan. Khalid Shaikh Mohammed, the self-described mastermind of the September 11 attacks, confessed to Pearl's murder and is awaiting trial in New York. Yet, in explaining the importance of the bill, Obama did not whisper a word about the role of al Qaeda or Islamist radicalism in Pearl's death.

The Obama administration, like the liberal base of its party, clings to a secular vision of global affairs with the discipline of a Benedictine monk. Tom Farr, a former State Department official and visiting professor at Georgetown University, argues that the United States is thus failing to advance practical alternatives to militant Islam. "If we have learned anything in Iraq," he writes, "it should have been that religion drives culture, for good or ill, that we did not fully comprehend that reality, and that we still have not absorbed its implications for the democracy project."

To the degree that Obama believes in promoting democracy, his efforts will flounder if they continue to lack moral realism: a deep sense of the corruptibility of religion. "The fine flower of unholiness," wrote C.S. Lewis, "can grow only in the close neighborhood of the Holy."

Nevertheless, just as religion can be a source of radicalism, it also can inspire political reform. If the goal is to win hearts and minds, then the religious ideals which move many hearts and minds around the world must be taken into account. There are countless Muslim reformers, living under despotic regimes, who cannot imagine a just society without a spiritual foundation. There are many non-Muslim minorities in these nations—Christians, Jews, Bahá'ís, and others—who are prepared to work with them, if only they enjoyed the same political rights as their Muslim neighbors. Neither the militant secularist nor the political realist has anything to say to them.

It is time for American diplomacy to shake off its doubts. The danger for U.S. diplomats now is not the start of a holy war, but a secular retreat that allows the fanatics to win.

"The United States, like any nation—but especially because it is a great power—simply has interests that do not always cohere with its values."

The Tragedy of U.S. Foreign Policy

Robert D. Kaplan

In the following viewpoint, Robert D. Kaplan argues that it is a mistake to think of morality as the main issue guiding foreign policy. Kaplan contends that one of the United States' overriding interests is to remain the dominant world power, and to be serious about this goal entails recognizing that foreign policy must adhere to realism. Kaplan is chief geopolitical analyst for global intelligence firm Stratfor, nonresident senior fellow at the Center for a New American Security, and author of The Revenge of Geography: What the Map Tells Us About Coming Conflicts and the Battle Against Fate.

As you read, consider the following questions:

1. According to the author, prior to the current humanitarian calls to intervene in Syria, humanitarians demanded military intervention where?

2. According to Kaplan, what was the primary goal of US involvement in World War II?

3. For what reason does Kaplan dispute the claim that the US interventions in Bosnia and Kosovo support a humanitarian foreign policy?

For over two years, the civil war in Syria has been synonymous with cries of moral urgency. *Do Something!* shout those who demand the United States intervene militarily to set the situation there to rights, even as the battle lines now comprise hundreds of regime and rebel groupings and the rebels have started fighting each other. *Well, then*, shout the moral interventionists, *if only we had intervened earlier!*

Syria is not unique. Before Syria, humanitarians in 2011 demanded military intervention in Libya, even though the regime of Muammar Gaddafi had given up its nuclear program and had been cooperating for years with Western intelligence agencies. In fact, the United States and France did lead an intervention, and Libya today is barely a state, with Tripoli less a capital than the weak point of imperial-like arbitration for far-flung militias, tribes, and clans, while nearby Saharan entities are in greater disarray because of weapons flooding out of Libya.

The 1990s were full of calls for humanitarian intervention: in Rwanda, which tragically went unheeded; and in Bosnia and Kosovo where interventions, while belated, were by and large successful. Free from the realpolitik necessities of the Cold War, humanitarians have in the past two decades tried to reduce foreign policy to an aspect of genocide prevention. Indeed, the Nazi Holocaust is only one lifetime removed from our own—a nanosecond in human history—and so post–Cold War foreign policy now rightly exists in the shadow of it. The codified upshot has been R2P: the "Responsibility to Protect," the mantra of humanitarians.

But American foreign policy cannot merely be defined by R2P and *Never Again!* Statesmen can only rarely be concerned with humanitarian interventions and protecting human rights to the exclusion of other considerations. The United States, like any nation—but especially because it is a great power—simply has interests that do not always cohere with its values. That is tragic, but it is a tragedy that has to be embraced and accepted.

What are those overriding interests? The United States, as the dominant power in the Western Hemisphere, must always prevent any other power from becoming equally dominant in the Eastern Hemisphere. Moreover, as a liberal maritime power, the United States must seek to protect the sea lines of communication that enable world trade. It must also seek to protect both treaty and de facto allies, and especially their access to hydrocarbons. These are all interests that, while not necessarily contradictory to human rights, simply do not operate in the same category.

Because the United States is a liberal power, its interests—even when they are not directly concerned with human rights—are generally moral. But they are only secondarily moral. For seeking to adjust the balance of power in one's favor has been throughout history an amoral enterprise pursued by both liberal and illiberal powers. Nevertheless, when a liberal power like the United States pursues such a goal in the service of preventing war among major states, it is acting morally in the highest sense.

A telling example of this tension—one that gets to the heart of why *Never Again!* and R2P cannot always be the operative words in statesmanship—was recently provided by the foreign affairs expert Leslie H. Gelb. Gelb noted that after Saddam Hussein had gassed close to seven thousand Kurds to death in northern Iraq in 1988, even a "truly ethical" secretary of state, George Shultz, committed a "moral outrage." For Shultz basically ignored the incident and continued supporting Saddam in his war against Iran, because weakening Iran—not protecting the citizens of Iraq—was the primary American *interest* at the time.

So was Shultz acting immorally? Not completely, I believe. Shultz was operating under a different morality than the one normally applied by humanitarians. His was a public morality; not a private one. He and the rest of the Reagan administration had a responsibility to the hundreds of millions of Americans under their charge. And while these millions were fellow countrymen, they were more crucially voters and citizens, essentially strangers who did not know Shultz or Reagan personally, but who had entrusted the two men with their interests. And the American public's interest clearly dictated that of the two states, Iran and Iraq, Iran at the time constituted the greater threat. In protecting the public interest of even a liberal power, a statesman cannot always be nice; or humane.

I am talking here of a morality of public outcomes, rather than one of private intentions. By supporting Iraq, the Reagan administration succeeded in preventing Iran in the last years of the Cold War from becoming a regional hegemon. That was an outcome convenient to U.S. interests, even if the morality of the affair was ambiguous, given that Iraq's regime was at the time the more brutal of the two.

In seeking good outcomes, policy makers are usually guided by constraints: a realistic awareness of what, for instance, the United States should and should not do, given its finite resources. After all, the United States had hundreds of thousands of troops tied down in Europe and Northeast Asia during the Cold War, and thus had to contain Iran through the use of a proxy, Saddam's Iraq. That was not entirely cynical: It was an intelligent use of limited assets in the context of a worldwide geopolitical struggle.

The problem with a foreign policy driven foremost by *Never Again!* is that it ignores limits and the availability of resources. World War II had the secondary, moral effect of saving what was left of European Jewry. Its primary goal and effect was to restore the European and Asian balance of power in a manner tolerable to the United States—something that the Nazis and the Japanese fascists had overturned. Of course, the Soviet Union wrested control of Eastern Europe for nearly half a century following the war. But again, limited resources necessitated an American alliance with the mass murderer [Joseph] Stalin against the mass murderer [Adolf] Hitler. It is because of such awful choices and attendant compromises—in which morality intertwines with amorality—that humanitarians will frequently be disappointed with the foreign policy of even the most heroic administrations.

World War II certainly involved many hideous compromises and even mistakes on President Franklin D. Roosevelt's part. He got into the war in Europe very late; he did not bomb the rail tracks leading to the concentration camps; he might have been more aggressive with the Soviets on the question of Eastern Europe. But as someone representing the interests of the millions of strangers who had and had not voted for him, his aim was to defeat Nazi Germany and Imperial Japan in a manner that cost the fewest American soldiers' lives, and utilized the least amount of national resources. Saving the remnants of European Jewry was a moral consequence of his actions, but his methods contained tactical concessions that had fundamental amoral elements. Abraham Lincoln, for his part, brought mass suffering upon Southern civilians in the last phase of the Civil War in order to decisively defeat the South. The total war waged by generals William Tecumseh Sherman and Ulysses S. Grant was evidence of that. Simply put, there are actions of state that are the right things to do, even if they cannot be defined in terms of conventional morality.

Amoral goals, properly applied, do have moral effects. Indeed, in more recent times, President Richard Nixon and his secretary of state, Henry Kissinger, rushed arms to Israel following a surprise attack by Arab armies in the fall of 1973. The two men essentially told the American defense establishment that supporting Israel in its hour of need was the right thing to do, because it was necessary to send an unambiguous message of resolve to the Soviets and their Arab allies at a critical stage in the Cold War. Had they justified the arms transfers purely in terms of helping embattled post-Holocaust Jewry—rather than in terms of power politics as they did—it would have made for a much weaker argument in Washington, where officials rightly had American interests at heart more than Israeli ones. George McGovern was possibly a more ethical man than either Nixon or Kissinger. But had he been elected president in 1972, would he have acted so wisely and so decisively during the 1973 Middle East war? The fact is, individual perfection, as [Niccolò] Machiavelli knew, is not necessarily synonymous with public virtue.

Then there is the case of Deng Xiaoping. Deng approved the brutal suppression of students at Beijing's Tiananmen Square in 1989. For that he is not respected among humanitarians in the West. But the consolidation of Communist Party control that followed the clampdown allowed for Deng's methodical, market-oriented reforms to continue for a generation in China. Perhaps never before in recorded economic history have so many people seen such a dramatic rise in living standards, with an attendant rise in personal (if not political) freedoms in so short a time frame. Thus, Deng might be considered both a brutal Communist and the greatest man of the twentieth century. The morality of his life is complex.

The Bosnia and Kosovo interventions of 1995 and 1999 are frequently held out as evidence that the United States is most effective when it acts according to its humanitarian values—never mind its amoral interests. But those who make that argument neglect to mention that the two successful interventions were eased by the fact that America operated in the Balkans with the balance of power strongly in its favor. Russia in the 1990s was weak and chaotic under Boris Yeltsin's incompetent rule, and thus temporarily less able to challenge the United States in a region where historically the czars and commissars had exerted considerable sway. However, Russia, even in the 1990s, still exerted considerable sway in the Caucasus, and thus a Western response to halt ethnic cleansing there during the same decade was not even considered. More broadly, the 1990s allowed for ground interventions in the Balkans because the international climate was relatively benign: China was only just beginning its naval expansions (endangering our Pacific allies) and September 11 still lay in the future. Truly, beyond many a moral response lies a question of power that cannot be explained wholly in terms of morality.

Thus, to raise morality as a sole arbiter is ultimately not to be serious about foreign policy. R2P must play as large a role as realistically possible in the affairs of state. But it cannot ultimately dominate. Syria is the current and best example of this. U.S. power is capable of many things, yet putting a complex and war-torn Islamic society's house in order is not one of them. In this respect, our tragic experience in Iraq is indeed relevant. Quick fixes like a no-fly zone and arming the rebels may topple Syrian dictator Bashar al-Assad, but that might only make President Barack Obama culpable in midwifing to power a Sunni-Jihadist regime, even as ethnic cleansing of al-Assad's Alawites commences. At least at this late juncture, without significant numbers of Western boots on the ground for a significant period—something for which there is little public support—the likelihood of a better, more stable regime emerging in Damascus is highly questionable. Frankly, there are just no easy answers here, especially as the pro-Western regime in Jordan is threatened by continued Syrian violence. R2P applied in 2011 in Syria might actually have yielded a better strategic result: It will remain an unknowable.

Because moralists in these matters are always driven by righteous passion, whenever you disagree with them, you are by definition immoral and deserve no quarter; whereas realists, precisely because they are used to conflict, are less likely to overreact to it. Realists know that passion and wise policy rarely flow together. (The late diplomat Richard Holbrooke was a stunning exception to this rule.) Realists adhere to the belief of the mid-twentieth-century University of Chicago political scientist Hans Morgenthau, who wrote that "one must work with" the base forces of human nature, "not against them." Thus, realists accept the human material at hand in any given place, however imperfect that material may be. To wit, you can't go around toppling regimes just because you don't like them. Realism, adds Morgenthau, "appeals to historical precedent rather than to abstract principles [of justice] and aims at the realization of the lesser evil rather than of the absolute good."

No group of people internalized such tragic realizations better than Republican presidents during the Cold War. Dwight Eisenhower, Richard Nixon, Ronald Reagan and George H.W. Bush all practiced amorality, realism, restraint and humility in foreign affairs (if not all the time). It is their sensibility that should guide us now. Eisenhower represented a pragmatic compromise within the Republican Party between isolationists and rabid anti-Communists. All of these men supported repressive, undemocratic regimes in the Third World in support of a favorable balance of power against the Soviet Union. Nixon accepted the altogether brutal regimes in the Soviet Union and "Red" China as legitimate, even as he balanced one against the other. Reagan spoke the Wilsonian language of moral rearmament, even as he awarded the key levers of bureaucratic power to realists like Caspar Weinberger, George Shultz and Frank Carlucci, whose effect regarding policy was to temper Reagan's rhetoric. The elder Bush did not break relations with China after the Tiananmen uprising;

nor did he immediately pledge support for Lithuania, after that brave little country declared its independence—for fear of antagonizing the Soviet military. It was caution and restraint on Bush's part that helped bring the Cold War to a largely peaceful—and, therefore, moral—conclusion. In some of these policies, the difference between amorality and morality was, to paraphrase Joseph Conrad in *Lord Jim*, no more than "the thickness of a sheet of paper."

And that is precisely the point: foreign policy at its best is subtle, innovative, contradictory, and truly bold only on occasion, aware as its most disciplined practitioners are of the limits of American power. That is heartrending, simply because calls to alleviate suffering will in too many instances go unanswered. For the essence of tragedy is not the triumph of evil over good, so much as the triumph of one good over another that causes suffering.

Periodical and Internet Sources Bibliography

The following articles have been selected to supplement the diverse views presented in this chapter.

Nada Bakos	"Humility Now!," *Foreign Policy*, April 2, 2013.
Zack Beauchamp	"How to Think About the Future of American Foreign Policy," *ThinkProgress*, October 30, 2013.
Ilan Berman	"Another Surrender in the War on Ideas," *American*, August 13, 2012.
Ronald Brownstein	"How to Reinvent Foreign Aid," *National Journal*, June 20, 2013.
Daniel Jonah Goldhagen	"The Sudan Crisis: Obama's Hypocrisy and Culpability," *New Republic*, June 22, 2011.
Lawrence J. Haas	"Obama's Retreat from the War on Terror," *U.S. News & World Report*, May 28, 2013.
Daniel Larison	"Seeking a Foreign Policy of Restraint and Humility," *American Conservative*, March 22, 2013.
John J. Mearsheimer	"Imperial by Design," *National Interest*, January/February 2011.
Ankit Panda	"Why Are Americans Suddenly Pessimistic About the Future of US Power?," *Diplomat*, December 5, 2013.
Tom Rogan	"The American Choice in International Affairs," *National Review Online*, September 9, 2013.
David Rohde	"Why Economics, Not Military Might, Is the Future of Foreign Policy," *Atlantic*, December 5, 2013.

For Further Discussion

Chapter 1

1. Both the Pew Research Center and the Chicago Council (as recounted by Gregory Holyk and Dina Smeltz) conducted surveys about US engagement around the world. Are the results consistent with each other, or do the results contradict each other? Defend your answer.

2. Micah Zenko believes that an international framework should govern drone strikes, whereas Arthur Herman and John Yoo say that international law should not be used to regulate the use of drones. Who do you think has the better argument? Thoroughly explain your answer, giving specific reasons.

Chapter 2

1. Ben Voth argues that there were four key accomplishments of the war in Iraq. Explain how Jamie Tarabay would dispute at least one of the accomplishments, using direct textual support for your claim.

2. Frederick W. Kagan and Kimberly Kagan argue that success is still possible in the war in Afghanistan. Does Conn Hallinan deny this? Why, or why not?

3. Both David Ignatius and Ammar Abdulhamid support US military intervention in Syria. What is their main disagreement on the issue? Support your answer with direct quotes from the respective viewpoints.

Chapter 3

1. Both Laurie Garrett and Charles Krauthammer support foreign aid by the United States. How do they differ in their justifications for aid? Explain.

2. David Meir-Levi and Doug Bandow take opposing views

on the issue of American foreign aid to Israel. Meir-Levi claims that the money is a good investment. What do you think Bandow would say in response to this particular argument? Explain your reasoning.

Chapter 4

1. How might James Traub respond to claims that it is a mistake to expect nations to reflect individual virtues such as humility? Explain your reasoning.

2. Robert D. Kaplan claims that it is a mistake to let morality guide US foreign policy decisions, arguing that the United States has interests that do not always cohere with its values. Using Kaplan's reasoning, under what circumstances should the United States intervene in a country where genocide is occurring? Do you agree with Kaplan's reasoning? Why, or why not?

Organizations to Contact

The editors have compiled the following list of organizations concerned with the issues debated in this book. The descriptions are derived from materials provided by the organizations. All have publications or information available for interested readers. The list was compiled on the date of publication of the present volume; the information provided here may change. Be aware that many organizations take several weeks or longer to respond to inquiries, so allow as much time as possible.

American Enterprise Institute (AEI)
1150 Seventeenth Street NW, Washington, DC 20036
(202) 862-5800 • fax: (202) 862-7177
e-mail: info@aei.org
website: www.aei.org

The American Enterprise Institute (AEI) is a private, nonpartisan, nonprofit institution dedicated to research and education on issues of government, politics, economics, and social welfare. AEI sponsors research and publishes materials defending the principles of American freedom and democratic capitalism, through projects such as its Center for Defense Studies. AEI publishes the *American*, its online magazine, and numerous policy studies.

American Foreign Policy Council (AFPC)
509 C Street NE, Washington, DC 20002
(202) 543-1006 • fax: (202) 543-1007
e-mail: afpc@afpc.org
website: www.afpc.org

The American Foreign Policy Council (AFPC) is a nonprofit organization dedicated to bringing information to those who make or influence the foreign policy of the United States. AFPC provides resources to members of Congress, the executive branch, and the policy-making community. AFPC publishes policy papers and numerous in-house bulletins, including *China Reform Monitor, Eurasia Security Watch*, and *Iran Democracy Monitor*.

American Israel Public Affairs Committee (AIPAC)

251 H Street NW, Washington, DC   20001
(202) 639-5200 • fax: (202) 347-4918
website: www.aipac.org

The American Israel Public Affairs Committee (AIPAC) is a pro-Israel lobby that works to strengthen the US-Israeli relationship. AIPAC works with both Democratic and Republican political leaders to enact public policy that supports Israel. Among its publications are *Near East Report, Defense Digest*, and issue memos such as "American Leadership Keeps Us Safe: The Case for Foreign Aid."

Brookings Institution

1775 Massachusetts Avenue NW, Washington, DC   20036
(202) 797-6000
e-mail: communications@brookings.edu
website: www.brookings.edu

The Brookings Institution is a nonprofit public policy organization that conducts independent research. The Brookings Institution uses its research to provide recommendations that advance the goals of strengthening American democracy, fostering social welfare and security, and securing a cooperative international system. Brookings publishes a variety of books, reports, and journals, including the report *The United States and the Middle East: Avoiding Miscalculation and Preparing for Conflict*.

Cato Institute

1000 Massachusetts Avenue NW, Washington, DC   20001-
5403
(202) 842-0200 • fax: (202) 842-3490
website: www.cato.org

The Cato Institute is a public policy research organization dedicated to the principles of individual liberty, limited government, free markets, and peace. The Cato Institute aims to provide clear, thoughtful, and independent analysis on vital public policy issues. The institute publishes numerous policy studies, two quarterly journals—*Regulation* and the *Cato Journal*—and the bimonthly *Cato Policy Report*.

Center for Security Policy

1901 Pennsylvania Avenue NW, Suite 201, Washington, DC 20006
(202) 835-9077
e-mail: info@securefreedom.org
website: www.centerforsecuritypolicy.org

The Center for Security Policy is a nonprofit, nonpartisan, national security organization that works to establish successful national security policies through the use of diplomatic, informational, military, and economic strength. The center believes that America's national power must be preserved and properly used because it holds a unique global role in maintaining peace and stability. The center publishes periodic *Occasional Papers* and articles, all of which are available at its website.

Center for Strategic and International Studies (CSIS)

1616 Rhode Island Avenue NW, Washington, DC 20036
(202) 887-0200 • fax: (202) 775-3199
website: www.csis.org

The Center for Strategic and International Studies (CSIS) is a nonprofit organization that provides strategic insights and bipartisan policy solutions to decision makers. CSIS conducts research and analysis for decision makers in government, international institutions, the private sector, and civil society. CSIS publishes reports, books, commentary, and the *Washington Quarterly*.

Council on Foreign Relations (CFR)

The Harold Pratt House, 58 East Sixty-Eighth Street, New York, NY   10065
(212) 434-9400 • fax: (212) 434-9800
e-mail: communications@cfr.org
website: www.cfr.org

The Council on Foreign Relations (CFR) is an independent, nonpartisan membership organization, think tank, and publisher. CFR aims to be a resource for its members, government officials, business executives, journalists, educators and students, civic and religious leaders, and other interested citizens to help them better understand the world and the foreign policy choices facing the United States and other countries. CFR has numerous publications available at its website, including backgrounders, expert briefs, and the journal *Foreign Affairs*.

Foreign Policy Research Institute (FPRI)

1528 Walnut Street, Suite 610, Philadelphia, PA   19102
(215) 732-3774 • fax: (215) 732-4401
e-mail: fpri@fpri.org
website: www.fpri.org

The Foreign Policy Research Institute (FPRI) is an independent, nonprofit organization devoted to bringing the insights of scholarship to bear on the development of policies that advance US national interests. FPRI conducts research on pressing issues and long-term questions about international policy. The organization publishes the quarterly *Orbis*, several periodical bulletins, and numerous essays, all of which are available at its website.

Institute for Foreign Policy Analysis (IFPA)

675 Massachusetts Avenue, 10th Floor, Cambridge, MA   02139-3309
(617) 492-2116 • fax: (617) 492-8242
e-mail: mail@ifpa.org
website: www.ifpa.org

The Institute for Foreign Policy Analysis (IFPA) is an independent, nonpartisan research organization specializing in national security, foreign policy, and defense-planning issues. IFPA helps senior government policy makers, industry leaders, and officials in the public policy community make decisions about global security. IFPA publishes special reports and monographs on topics of importance to the foreign affairs and security studies communities.

Institute for Policy Studies (IPS)

1112 Sixteenth Street NW, Suite 600, Washington, DC   20036
(202) 234-9382
e-mail: info@ips-dc.org
website: www.ips-dc.org

The Institute for Policy Studies (IPS) is a community of public scholars and organizers linking peace, justice, and the environment in the United States and globally. IPS works with social movements to promote democracy and to challenge concentrated wealth, corporate influence, and military power. IPS publishes numerous reports available at its website and through Foreign Policy in Focus (FPIF), which aims to connect research and action.

Just Foreign Policy

4410 Massachusetts Avenue NW #290, Washington, DC 20016
(202) 448-2898
e-mail: info@justforeignpolicy.org
website: www.justforeignpolicy.org

Just Foreign Policy is an independent, nonpartisan membership organization that supports a multilateral approach to foreign relations that relies less on raw US military and economic power and more on international law and treaties, cooperation, and diplomacy. Just Foreign Policy aims to accelerate this transition through education, organization, and mobilization of concerned citizens. Just Foreign Policy has information about its many campaigns, such as Countdown to Drawdown, at its website.

US Department of Defense

1400 Defense Pentagon, Washington, DC   20301-1400
(703) 571-3343
website: www.defense.gov

The US Department of Defense is a governmental agency with the mission to provide the military forces needed to deter war and to protect the security of the United States. It is the federal department that supervises all agencies of the government related to national security and the armed forces. The website of the department contains news releases, photo essays, and reports, including "Progress Toward Security and Stability in Afghanistan."

Washington Institute for Near East Policy

1828 L Street NW, Suite 1050, Washington, DC   20036
(202) 452-0650 • fax: (202) 223-5364
website: www.washingtoninstitute.org

The Washington Institute for Near East Policy was established to advance a balanced and realistic understanding of American interests in the Middle East. It promotes an American engagement in the Middle East that is committed to strengthening alliances; nurturing friendships; and promoting security, peace, prosperity, and democracy for the people of the region. The institute publishes a variety of analysis available at its website.

Bibliography of Books

Stephen E.
Ambrose and
Douglas G.
Brinkley

Rise to Globalism: American Foreign Policy Since 1938. New York: Penguin Books, 2011.

Andrew J.
Bacevich

The Limits of Power: The End of American Exceptionalism. New York: Henry Holt, 2009.

Peter L. Bergen

The Longest War: The Enduring Conflict Between America and Al-Qaeda. New York: Free Press, 2011.

John Bolton

Surrender Is Not an Option: Defending America at the United Nations and Abroad. New York: Threshold Editions, 2008.

Michael Cox and
Doug Stokes, eds.

US Foreign Policy. New York: Oxford University Press, 2012.

Thomas Donnelly
and Frederick W.
Kagan, eds.

Lessons for a Long War: How America Can Win on New Battlefields. Washington, DC: AEI Press, 2010.

Tom Engelhardt

The American Way of War: How Bush's Wars Became Obama's. Chicago, IL: Haymarket Books, 2010.

Leslie H. Gelb

Power Rules: How Common Sense Can Rescue American Foreign Policy. New York: Harper, 2009.

Richard N. Haass — *Foreign Policy Begins at Home: The Case for Putting America's House in Order.* New York: Basic Books, 2013.

George C. Herring — *From Colony to Superpower: U.S. Foreign Relations Since 1776.* New York: Oxford University Press, 2011.

Steven W. Hook — *U.S. Foreign Policy: The Paradox of World Power.* Los Angeles, CA: Sage/CQ Press, 2013.

Chalmers Johnson — *Dismantling the Empire: America's Last Best Hope.* New York: Metropolitan Books, 2010.

Robert Kagan — *The Return of History and the End of Dreams.* New York: Vintage, 2009.

Joyce P. Kaufman — *A Concise History of U.S. Foreign Policy.* Lanham, MD: Rowman & Littlefield, 2013.

Parag Khanna — *The Second World: How Emerging Powers Are Redefining Global Competition in the Twenty-First Century.* New York: Random House, 2009.

Jeffrey S. Lantis — *US Foreign Policy in Action.* Chichester, West Sussex: John Wiley & Sons, 2013.

Catherine Lutz, ed. — *The Bases of Empire: The Global Struggle Against U.S. Military Posts.* New York: New York University Press, 2009.

Jack F. Matlock Jr. *Superpower Illusions: How Myths and False Ideologies Led America Astray—And How to Return to Reality.* New Haven, CT: Yale University Press, 2011.

Alex Mintz and Karl DeRouen Jr. *Understanding Foreign Policy Decision Making.* New York: Cambridge University Press, 2010.

Vali Nasr *The Dispensable Nation: American Foreign Policy in Retreat.* New York: Anchor Books, 2014.

Tudor A. Onea *US Foreign Policy in the Post–Cold War Era: Restraint Versus Assertiveness from George H.W. Bush to Barack Obama.* New York: Palgrave Macmillan, 2013.

Kenneth M. Pollack *A Path Out of the Desert: A Grand Strategy for America in the Middle East.* New York: Random House, 2009.

Christopher A. Preble *The Power Problem: How American Military Dominance Makes Us Less Safe, Less Prosperous, and Less Free.* Ithaca, NY: Cornell University Press, 2009.

Peter H. Schuck and James Q. Wilson, eds. *Understanding America: The Anatomy of an Exceptional Nation.* New York: PublicAffairs, 2009.

Strobe Talbott	*The Great Experiment: The Story of Ancient Empires, Modern States, and the Quest for a Global Nation.* New York: Simon & Schuster, 2009.
Ethan Watters	*Crazy Like Us: The Globalization of the American Psyche.* New York: Free Press, 2011.
Fareed Zakaria	*The Post-American World.* New York: W.W. Norton, 2009.

Index

A